A STRAIGHTFORWARD GUIDE TO GETTING THE BEST OUT OF YOUR RETIREMENT

PATRICK GRANT

Editor: Roger Sproston

D1390532

Straightforward Guides

© Straightforward Co Ltd 2019

ISBN
978-1-84716-937-2

Printed by 4edge Co Ltd www.4edge.co.uk

Cover design by Straightforward Graphics

Whilst every effort has been made to ensure that the information contained within this book is correct at the time of going to press, the author and publisher can take no responsibility for the errors or omissions contained within.

Contents

Chapter 1.
When You Retire   6

Chapter 2.
Taking Holidays   16

Chapter 3.
Managing Your Home   24

Chapter 4.
Raising Capital from Your Home   40

Chapter 5.
Extras Because of Age   46

Chapter 6.
Future Care Options   54

Chapter 7
Income Tax-How it affects you   64

Chapter 8.
Making a Will   75

.

Part Two: Finances After Retirement-Pensions

Chapter 9.
Pensions and Planning for the Future   80

Chapter 10. How much income is needed in retirement   87

Chapter 11.
Sources of Pension   95

Chapter 12.
Private Pension Savings Generally   101

Chapter 13.
Choosing a Personal Pension Plan   107

Chapter 14.
Pensions and Benefits for Dependants   116

Chapter 15.
Pensions, options for Retirement   120
and tax implications

Chapter 16.
Reaching Retirement Age   135

Useful addresses

Index

****

Introduction

Most people start to seriously think about their retirement when they reach their late 50's /early 60's. They think about how they can afford their retirement and how they can best spend their time. On average, a third of a person's lifetime is spent in retirement and it is a great opportunity to take up the many things that you have not had the time for.

Of course, it is the case that many people have a very clear idea about what they want to do and how much it is all going to cost. There is suddenly time to do everything that you have wanted, within reason and within financial limits. There are, however, hidden problems that can surface when a person retires. One of these is personal relationships. Retirement can cause stress in people's relationships as you now spend a lot more time together or one partner retires and wants to embark on different projects whilst the other is still working.

People who live alone may worry about losing the day-to-day companionship that goes with the workplace. People also worry about how they may cope as they get older and ill health begins to surface.

This book updated to **2019**, attempts to cover all areas relating to retirement. The first chapters deal with more personal matters, including management of the home and future care options whilst the latter chapters deal with more financial issues, such as pensions and benefits. All in all, the reader will benefit from this highly readable book which is packed with information.

Patrick Grant

Ch. 1

When You Retire

Although people generally look forward to retirement, it is true to say that, in the absence of any grand plans, the experience of being at home can take some adjusting to.

Being on your own

There are increasing numbers of people who find themselves alone when they retire. Many people like being single and have planned their lives around this. Although it is true that having a partner can mean that you have someone to be with, go on holiday with and do many other things with, some people like to do these things either on their own or perhaps with another member of the family.

However, many people on their own also hope that they can find a partner in retirement, someone to share life with. This can be more difficult for women than men. Older women outnumber men, and men may be on the lookout for a younger partner.

The truth is that, in older age, many people will find it difficult to find a partner. The opportunities get less and less. One option is to contact a marriage bureau or to enrol on a dating site online or to go to a dating agency. If you are thinking about contacting a dating agency, particularly for the first time, make sure that you know exactly what you are looking for-a long term relationship or something less committed. Also, beware! As with many things there are a lot of bogus online dating agencies around. Make sure that you do your research well.

If you live alone, and don't intend to look for a partner, then you might want to develop your ties in the community. A sense of belonging, of community, is very important so as not to get too isolated and so as to ensure that someone will always look out for you.

Your partner

If you are retiring and have a partner, you will need to involve them in your retirement plans. This may sound obvious but by no means do all people communicate with each other clearly when it comes to life after retirement and problems can occur. You will have to decide how to cope being with each other all the time, after spending so much time apart when working. If you think that you may need help with the transition to retirement then you should contact RELATE who specialise in this area. Many people see RELATE as dealing only with marital breakdown but they specialise in marital problems generally, or potential problems. See useful addresses at the back of this book.

Sexual relations

It doesn't follow that, as people get older so their sex life diminishes or the desire goes away. It is a fact that many people enjoy active sexual relations for many years after they retire. This aspect of life is just as important to older people as for younger couples.

Most people are able to enjoy sexual relations throughout their lives. However, when people get older sexual expression can take many forms. The importance of an orgasm, for example, may diminish. The main thing is that two people enjoy sex in their own way. As long as fulfilment is gained then this is all that matters. Growing older can bring some advantages in relation to sex. Once a woman is past the menopause then the fear of getting pregnant disappears. For many women, the fact that their partner takes longer to reach orgasm is a definite bonus. Also, when people enter the phase of retirement there is generally more time to enjoy and explore sexual relations. It goes without saying that sexual relationships don't just involve women. Partners of the same sex equally enjoy sexual relationships as they get older.

Enhancing your sex life

Although, as discussed, people of all ages enjoy active sex lives, it is true to say that for some older people sex becomes less and less frequent. Some people eventually give up altogether, for a variety of reasons, the main one being the loss of interest in one's partner. This should also be handled in the right way. Life together doesn't have to be dominated by sex. If both parties feel comfortable without sex then so be it. The important thing is to maintain good relationships.

There are, however, a few tips which may help stimulate your sex life. A complete change of scene can be exciting. Making love in a hotel room, making love at different times of the day, watching a film can all be aides to a better sex life. You might also want to consider sexual therapy, such as Sensate Focusing, which was pioneered in America by Masters and Johnson. The treatment consists of three phases. During the first phase the couple will be tactile, told to stroke each others bodies, apart from the genitals, telling each other what they like or dislike. At this stage, the therapist will recommend that there is no sexual intercourse. The second stage allows genital stimulation and the third stage full intercourse. If you feel that you would like to explore sexual therapy more, either through the NHS or privately you should contact the British Association for Sexual and Marital Therapy, (BASMT) www.basmt.org.uk address at the end of the book. Age UK also has a publication called Intimate Relations: Living and Loving in Later Life.

Opportunities Available

When you retire you will find that you have a lot more time on your hands, and it is yours to do as you choose. There are many opportunities. People retiring today live longer and will spend, or could spend, almost as much time retired as working. The fact that you will have so much time in retirement means that it is very important that you make the best use of it.

Learning opportunities

When you are retired you can set your goals however you want and one very useful way to use your time is to embark on a course of learning. You can study for your own personal satisfaction, studying, for example, politics and current affairs, philosophy or information technology. You may want to study informally or to obtain specific qualifications, such as GCSE. Another aspect of attending classes, either in the day or in the evening is that you will meet like-minded people. Because of age discrimination legislation contained within the 2010 Equalities Act, colleges and universities cannot refuse people entry to courses on the grounds of age, so the opportunities are limitless.

Informal ways of learning
Libraries

Libraries are a good place to find out what courses are happening in your area. Many libraries have also set up open learning centres where access to computers and the Internet is free, or at a very low cost.

Museums and galleries

As well as visiting museums and galleries you will also find that you can attend courses, lectures and various events organised by their education department for interested adults.

Radio and Television

Many radio and TV programmes are educational and certain programmes are dedicated to education, such as the Discovery channel. The Open University also has some very interesting programmes, based around their curriculum.

The Internet

This is, without doubt, a very convenient way to learn with almost every subject under the sun being available. If you are experienced and have used the Internet, and almost every one has nowadays, then you will have access to a rich variety of subjects.

If you are new to computers and would like to enrol on a course to learn more, you should try to find the one that best suits your needs. You might want to contact Digital Unite which is an organisation that offers computer training to the over 50's. It has a national network of older trainers:
www.digitalunite.com 0800 228 9272

In addition, many Age UK groups and organisations offer Internet and computer taster sessions in various community locations. You can contact Age UK's information line 0800 678 1602 or see the website www.ageuk.org.uk.

Attending classes locally

One of the most beneficial ways of learning is to attend a class near your home. There are a variety of classes, run by Local authority adult education services, Worker Educational Associations and others. The University of the Third Age is a useful organisation where activities are all arranged by members themselves, often being carried out in people's homes. The term 'university' is misleading, as no qualifications and exams are involved. There are more than 500 groups in the UK (see useful addresses at the back of the book). Learn Direct can also provide useful information about all areas of education and learning. You should phone 0800 101901 for more information or go onto their website www.learndirect.com.

Learning away from home

If you are not interested in committing yourself to a longer course then there is also the option of short residential courses, providing you can afford the fees. There are a variety of courses, from summer schools in colleges or universities and also field study centres. You can find information in local papers, travel agencies or in the Time to Learn Directory for which you have to pay. This is published twice a year by City and Guilds (see useful addresses at rear of book) or available online.

The Learning and Work Institute www.learningandwork.org.uk also offers useful information (see useful addresses).

Distance learning

'Distance learning' refers to learning by post, radio, email, television or the Internet. Although not everyone's cup of tea, it can be a useful form of learning. The main advantage is the flexibility as regards the contents and duration of the course.

The Open University www.open.ac.uk is perhaps the most famous of the distance learning organisations, where you can study for a degree (or not). The University offers a vast range of courses. See useful addresses for more information. The Open College of Arts www.oca-uk.com provides home study courses in a wide range of arts subjects, including music, photography and creative writing. The National Extension College (NEC) www.nec.ac.uk offers a wide variety of courses-from maths to bird watching including courses specifically geared to the needs of people who left school without qualifications and have not studied for some time, if at all.

The Association of British Correspondence Colleges www.homestudy.org.uk can provide lists of colleges and courses. For all of the above see useful addresses at the end of the book. For general information on distance learning courses, or to check the credentials of a course provider, contact the Open and Distance Learning Quality Council (ODLQC) www.odlqc.org.uk See useful addresses. In Scotland you should visit www.skillsdevelopmentscotland.co.uk

Taking a degree

Many universities and colleges will accept mature students on the basis of their experience rather than any formal paper qualifications. Many universities and colleges have foundation courses which can be taken prior to enrolling for a degree course. You will need to pay fees for taking a degree although if you are on a low income then you may qualify for assistance. Students of any age may apply for a student loan to help with tuition fees. However, you can only get a loan to help with living costs if you are under 60 years of age (England and Wales). In Scotland there are no fees for students:
www.mygov.scot/tuition-fee

The government website www.direct.gov.uk has helpful information about financing adult learning. General information about funding and concessions is available from Learndirect on 0800 101901.

For most people enrolling at the Open University, there is no need for any prior qualifications. However, OU students do not qualify for grants. An OU degree will usually take a little longer than a full time university based degree because of the nature of the learning process. It can take between 4-6 years to complete although this is dependent on the individual student.

For more information go to the OU website www.open.ac.uk or phone 0300 303 5303.

Getting involved in the community

Whilst people are at work, time for getting involved in community activities is limited. However, when you reach retirement age, there is adequate opportunity to get involved. Becoming involved in the local community can be very rewarding indeed and can be life changing in terms of who you meet and the activities that you get involved in.

Joining a local club or society

The best source of information concerning the type of club and the whereabouts is the local library. Before committing yourself to join any club you should take a look at the programme and attend an initial meeting as a guest. This will help you get an idea of the club/societies activities and to make a decision whether you want to give more of your time. Once involved you will meet many people with similar interests as you and this can be very rewarding.

Clubs for older people

Many of the larger employers will run clubs for ex-employees. These might be the civil service or NHS for example. Local Age UK's will provide information about different clubs and societies. In addition, active older people are always required as volunteers.

Women's clubs

The traditional idea of the women's institute, that of elderly and stuffy people is no longer anywhere near the truth. Today's WI's are very stimulating and can offer a range of activities for members. If you want more information contact the National Federation of Women's Institutes www. thewi.org.uk

Working as a volunteer

If you have the energy and the time then working as a volunteer can be very rewarding indeed. It can enable you to put to good use the skills that you have acquired at work, and to keep your hand in. Alternatively, it can give you the opportunity to do something totally different. The opportunities for doing voluntary work are endless. The following gives you some idea of the range of volunteering jobs. You could:

- Act as a guide or steward in a museum or stately home-the National Trust is always in need of volunteers
- Train to be a counsellor for organisations such as Relate, the Salvation Army or Victim Support
- Work with children and young people in a variety of settings
- Work with older people
- Help run a charity shop

- Become an advocate for a Citizens Advice Bureau.
- Become a magistrate or local councillor
- Sit on tribunals
- Participate in governing bodies such as a school governing body

You need to think about what you have to offer and what you really want to do and how much time you want to devote to voluntary work. As stated, it can be a very rewarding experience. You can find voluntary work through a variety of different mediums, such as Age Concern, libraries, The National Association For Voluntary and Community action (NAVCA), www.navca.org.uk volunteer centres, REACH www.reachskills.org.uk (which recruits volunteers with managerial and technical backgrounds) (see useful addresses) and the Retired and Senior Volunteer Programme www.csv-rsvp.org.uk which recruits volunteers over the age of 50. For more information about VSO (Volunteering Overseas) www.vso.org.uk see useful addresses. WORKING FOR A CHARITY www.wfac.org.uk offers training courses for people who want to volunteer in the charitable sector. See useful addresses.

****

Ch. 2

Taking Holidays

For most people who are working, holidays are confined to a few weeks a year. For those with children, holidays are usually limited to school holidays. However, once you are retired, money permitting, the choices are that much greater. There is more freedom and flexibility to plan holidays around off-peak times and also to stay away longer.

In addition, your priorities may change. Whereas when holidays were limited to a few weeks a year, sun, sand and sea may have been the destination. The possibilities are greater when you are retired.

The various holidays available
Activity holidays

In retirement you may be looking for something more stimulating than lying around on a beach (not that all people do that). Activity holidays have a special appeal and there are a number of possibilities.

Special-interest holidays

These are run by many operators. Details can be found in various media, such as special interest magazines or from Tourist Boards, Tourist Information Centres or from travel agents. These holidays cover a whole range of activities, including, for example, sports holidays, arts and crafts, outdoor pursuits, from canoeing to potholing, history tours, cooking, music and languages. These are just a few. There will almost certainly be something for everyone. Another option may be working holidays and the Conservation Volunteers www.greentraveller.co.uk is one example of an organisation that runs working holidays.

Town twinning exchanges with European counterpart towns are organised by local groups. If the town that you live in has a European Twin (or any other twin for that matter) you should approach your local council for more details.

Cycling holidays are one of the best ways to explore the countryside. Careful planning is needed here because obviously a lot will depend on your own personal capacity. Look at maps to ensure that you choose a route that isn't littered with steep hills. The National Cycling Charity, Cycling UK, www.cyclinguk. org. can provide information on cycling tours and routes in this country and abroad.

Walking holidays are another good way to see the countryside. The Ramblers Association www.ramblers.org.uk offer walking holidays. All holidays are carefully graded, ranging from the easy to the hard. The Ramblers can also assist if you would like a walking companion. Walking Women www.walkingwomen.com (see useful addresses) arranges women's walking holidays in the UK and abroad. Many women decide to go on their own.

Reunion holidays are well worth considering if you have relatives abroad. It might be worth joining a 'friendship club' – membership of Lion World Travel/Friendship Associations, for example, www.friendship-associations.co.uk entitles you to newsletters and discount flights for reunions in Australia, South Africa and New Zealand

Specialist tour operators

There are a growing number of tour operators offering specialist holidays for older people. Also, the Internet has a significant number of companies which offer specialist holidays. The Internet can also be cheaper. Also, local Age UK organisations and other groups run their own holidays, usually for more active older people.

Holidays for the single person

As we all know, on many fronts holidays can pose a number of problems for the single traveller. The main one, of course, is the absence of a companion. However, many holiday prices are built around two people travelling. The single person supplement can add a significant amount to a holiday.

One way around this is to go on an activity holiday, as detailed above. However, this isn't the ideal solution if you enjoy travelling around at your own pace on an itinerary designed by you. One company, Solitair Holidays www.solitairhols.co.uk offers singles holidays for weekends and longer breaks. There are also other companies that offer singles holidays and these can be best sourced on the internet.

Long-stay holidays

Long stay holidays are best taken when everyone else is working. They are cheaper and less overrun in these periods. April, May, September and October are the best months. Some special long-stay holidays are available during the winter months often at very cheap rates.

A long stay package may be the best option if it is the first time that you are embarking on such a holiday. It can also be a good bet if you are considering relocating abroad and want a taste of the country that you intend moving to. Some package holidays offer a substantial package of daytime activities and other excursions and also evening entertainment. You could take a car and rent a cottage or farmhouse in a village or right out in the country. Many holiday companies offer such packages to suit your needs.

Arranging your own holiday

If you are independent and prefer to stay that way then arranging your own holiday is obviously the best way to ensure that you can suit yourself.

Finding your own accommodation can be done as you go but it is better if you can plan in advance and book in advance. Again, arranging your own holiday can give you an insight into a place that you are thinking of moving to.

Home swapping

If you like the idea of a long stay holiday but can't really afford it, then home swapping may be a solution. You live in someone else's home for an agreed period of time, while they live in yours. When you arrange a swap, it is necessary to make certain arrangements, such as:

- Sort out who pays gas, electricity and phone bills, and also practicalities such as food in the freezer.
- Check the position with your insurance company regarding house contents whilst the visitors are living in the house.
- Leave instructions for domestic appliances and also other information about local buses, shops and facilities.

- Leave instructions concerning contacting contractors such as electricians, plumbers etc.
- Arrange for a neighbour to drop in and make sure all is well.

Try https://www.homeswapper.co.uk, and there are many more.

Voluntary work abroad

Another cheap way to have a long-stay holiday is to work abroad as a volunteer. Voluntary Services Overseas (VSO) takes volunteers up to the age of 75 years old. The usual spell abroad is two years. See useful addresses for more information.

Camping and caravanning

Camping and caravanning is very popular and offers greater flexibility when travelling around. This is just the sort of freedom that many people want. It also can work out cheaper in the long run once you have invested in all the equipment. If you have never been camping or caravanning, it is better to try a short package holiday first. Many people, in a fit of enthusiasm, have invested in expensive equipment only to never use it again. The same goes with camper vans. Always hire to begin with to see whether it is for you or not. If you enjoy the experience of camping or caravanning then you can always join the Camping and Caravan Club www.campingandcaravaningclub.co.uk

Medical care abroad

It is important, if you intend to travel abroad, that you are well aware of the healthcare situation in respective countries. You will need to check with your own doctor about the vaccinations that may be needed in different countries. You are covered by the NHS for medical treatment only while you are in the UK. If you fall ill whilst you are on holiday abroad, you may have to pay all or part of the cost of treatment. Obviously, medical insurance is a must.

There are special arrangements with many European countries by which you may be entitled to free or reduced cost state treatment. Notwithstanding BREXIT, which in 2019 seems to be imminent, these are still in force until further notice. To ensure that you receive this, you must get a European Health Insurance Card (EHIC) before you go away. The application form is available from main post offices or you can apply direct (see useful addresses).

Insurance

Holiday insurance should be taken out at the time that the holiday is booked because most companies give some cover in the event of cancellation. It may be harder to get insurance as you get older, as some companies impose terms or restrict insurance for those over 70. You need to shop around a range of insurers to get the best deal. You should make sure that you get all the cover that you need. Information about travel and holiday insurance is available on the Association of British Insurers (ABI) website www.abi.org.uk. Advice on taking a vehicle abroad is available from the AA or RAC.

Home security while you are away

In the ideal world you will not want to give the impression that your house is unoccupied. This is an invitation to burglars.

There are certain clues that can indicate an absent owner such as:

- Uncut grass
- Junk mail and free newspapers stuck in a letterbox

There is no real substitute for getting someone to keep an eye on your house for you. You can also use a 'home-sitting' service to look after your home whilst you are away. Always tell the insurance company that covers your property if you are going to be away for more than a few weeks. It may insist on extra security precautions if cover is to be maintained.

Can you afford a holiday?

There may be the possibility that you cannot afford a holiday. However, there may be some help available. Your local Age UK, local authority or Citizens Advice Bureau might know about charities in your area that can help.

Holidays for people with disabilities

There are a number of organisations that offer help to disabled people who are planning a holiday:

- Tourism for All www.tourismforall.co.uk is a charity that gives free information and advice on holidays for people with disabilities (see useful addresses)
- Local Age UK's sometimes organise holidays specifically for people who are frail or with disabilities.
- Local authority social services departments sometimes have their own accommodation for older and disabled people.
- The Royal Association for Disability Rights publishes a holiday guide Holidays in Britain and Ireland (see useful addresses)

- Charities such as Arthritis Care www.arthritiscare.org.uk and the Multiple Sclerosis Society www.mssociety.org.uk, for example, often provide information on holidays, and some have their own holiday homes or organise holidays for special groups.

Holidays for carers

If you are a carer and want a holiday break, it may be possible for a bed to be found in a hospital or local authority care home for the person that you care for. Ask your GP or local social services department. If you need a break yourself you can ask for a carers assessment. Vouchers may be available from the local authority to assist with the cost of care while you have your break. For more information contact Carers UK (see useful addresses).

****

Ch. 3

Managing Your Home

For many people, when reaching retirement age, an examination of the home that you live in is necessary. You may decide that the home that you live in will not be suitable in the future and you may want to change, probably to something smaller or in an area where you would rather be. It could even be abroad. There is also the option of moving to a care home, or housing for older people. All these options will be explored here. In addition, housing options for those with limited capital will be explored.

In many cases, those who retire and are considering selling their home will have lived in the property for many years, often raising children there. Over the years, many contacts and friendships will have formed in the community. Therefore, a number of questions need to be asked when considering selling up and moving, or giving up a rented home and moving:

- Do you still have an affinity to the area and is it likely to change in the future?
- Are you still near relatives and friends or have these patterns of friendship changed over the years and have your relatives moved on?
- Is your home expensive to run and maintain? How will this affect your finances in the future now that you are retired?

By releasing capital through the sale of your home and downsizing/moving area will this help your finances in the future? The sale of a larger home and the purchase of a smaller property or renting of a more age specific property can release capital which can be utilised as part of your pension plan or for liquid capital to give you a better quality of life in your retirement.

If you do decide to make a move then there are also a few important points to consider:

- Will the property be easy to convert as your needs change with age?
- Is the area that you are moving to convenient in terms of amenities, doctors, hospitals etc?
- Is the area quiet in the daytime or is it noisy?
- Is the property secure?

It may well be worth doing an analysis of the good and bad points of your current home before making any decision. Of course, it may well be that, notwithstanding the good points of your current home, it is simply too large to continue to occupy, too expensive and a move is essential. When making your decision, it is well worth looking at Housing Options for Older People (HOOP). www.housingcare.org which is a self-assessment form for people wondering whether to move. The form is available from the Elderly Accommodation Council www.eac.org.uk (see useful addresses)

Moving to retirement housing

Retirement housing falls into several categories depending on need. It is usually available for those over 60, although there are a number of schemes which are designed for the over 55's. These schemes usually comprise of a number of flats, some with a resident warden, most with an alarm system connected to a central base which can summon help in the event of an emergency. There are many different types of scheme. You basically get what you pay for and those with a number of services will have a corresponding service charge to match.

Many schemes will have a communal laundry and also, in some cases, a kitchen and dining room where meals can be purchased. A guest room is also usually available.

You may decide that sheltered housing (as it is usually referred to) is the ideal choice for you. The presence of a scheme manager might be reassuring and the company of others in a communal area may suit you. However, before deciding on this option, you need to weigh up the advantages and disadvantages of more sheltered housing. There will be the feeling of being 'herded' together and the loss of independence. If you feel like this you should also see whether you can receive the range of services offered in sheltered housing in your own home.

Renting retirement housing

Most retirement homes for rent are provided by local authorities and housing associations, although not all. There are also a number of schemes offered by the larger private providers although they have to manage to high standards set by local authorities. The Elderly Accommodation Counsel can offer advice.

Purchasing a retirement home

Retirement housing for sale is usually constructed by private developers although an increasing number of housing associations are also providing this type of accommodation now. Once all the properties in a scheme have been sold then the management of the scheme will be handed over to a private management company or housing association. The management organisation will be responsible for the overall management and service provision. Most retirement homes are sold on a leasehold basis with an annual ground rent (typically £250 per annum) and with a service charge that will depend on what services you are being provided. These can range from skeletal to intensive depending on your requirements.

When purchasing a retirement home it is always wise to buy off a developer who is registered with the National House Building Council (NHBC). The NHBC has a code of practice applying to all retirement homes built after 1st April 1990. If you are seriously considering buying into, or renting retirement housing there are a number of important points to consider:

- As with all housing, is the property in a convenient location and will it cater for your needs when you get older?
- What are the facilities within the scheme?
- Will the new property take your existing furniture or will you have to sell this and buy new?
- Most important, are the managing agents experienced in managing retirement housing?
- Who runs the management association, will leaseholders have a say in running it?
- How much is the service charge and what does it cover?
- What is the ground rent?
- What are the other expenses involved?

- If there is a separate sinking fund for future major repairs how do residents contribute to it?
- What are the arrangements for resale?
- Does the lease cover what will happen if your health deteriorates whilst you are in the property?
- Who owns the freehold of the property?

The above questions should be answered by the information provided in the Purchasers Information Pack which must be provided. The NHBC Code of Practice sets out what information should be in the pack.

Although many basic rights of leaseholders have been developed over the years and are enshrined in law, the lease is still paramount in terms of what services you will receive, how they are provided and what they will cost.

Invaluable advice for those living in, or intending to move into, retirement housing is provided by First Stop www.firststopcareadvice.org.uk See useful addresses. First Stop provides useful written information, prepared in conjunction with The Leasehold Advisory Service called Leasehold Retirement Housing, Your Rights and Remedies.

Options for people with limited resources

Most retirement housing is sold, as with other housing, at full market value. It follows that when you sell you get the current market value. When you sell your own property and look for retirement housing, you might find yourself in a position of not being able to buy elsewhere. This has particularly been the case in the last few years of spiralling house prices and the general distortions of the British housing scene. If you are in the position of not being able to buy elsewhere after selling your home, there are a few options to consider.

Shared ownership housing

Some housing associations and, increasingly due to over-development, private developers, run schemes where you can part buy and part-rent. There are all sorts of names used to describe this model, such as homebuy, but essentially it is what it always has been, shared ownership. In this case, you buy a percentage of the value of the property, say 25%, and then you rent the other 75%. On top of this there will be a service charge (with flats and some houses). It is not the cheapest way to obtain housing but it ensures that you get your foot on the property ladder. You should make enquiries of your local housing association which will point you in the right direction.

Lifetime lease

Some companies offer a lifetime lease, or occupancy, which means that you buy the right to live in your home for the rest of your life. The properties are sold below the market price but you will probably get very little back if you need to move again. They are also known as life interest plans.

To find out if there are any schemes in your area you should contact your local council or the Elderly Accommodation Council (address at back of this book).

Moving to rented accommodation

If you wish to move home but cannot afford to buy elsewhere, then renting privately is another option. Rented accommodation is provided in the main by local authorities, housing associations and the private sector. It is easier to rent privately than through the public sector as there is quite often a long waiting list for property and your capital may rule you out. However, tenancies in the private sector are usually insecure in that they are let out on assured shorthold tenancies which usually have a fixed duration of six months. If you wish to rent privately you should always try to go for a minimum term of twelve months. Property investors who are holding onto property for a longer term will usually be willing to do this as they are always on the lookout for a good tenant who will pay their rent. Remember, from June 1st 2019, lettings agents and landlords are not allowed to charge fees when letting property, although there are certain fees a landlord can charge during the course of a tenancy. Also, tenants deposits are capped at 5 weeks. For more information on this area go to www.arla.co.uk/letting-agent-fees.asp

Options for existing public sector tenants

If you are already a local authority or housing association tenant, and wish to relocate to another area, you may be able to exchange your home with another council or association tenant. This will be dependant on whether the exchange is suitable, taking into account the size of the respective properties or whether any possession orders or rent arrears exist. The council or association cannot unreasonably refuse the exchange. You will find details of exchange schemes at your local council or by making enquiries to your local housing association. The Internet also has details of several national exchange schemes.

Right to buy

If you have been a council tenant for five years or more you will usually have the right to purchase your property at a discount. The discounts are now more generous, at the time of writing.

You won't usually be entitled to buy your home if you are a housing association tenant, although there are some exceptions such as stock transfers from local authorities to associations where the right to buy is preserved. In addition, the current government has promised to extend right to buy to housing association tenants. You won't, however, be able to exercise the right to buy in housing that is exclusively reserved for elderly people.

Moving to specialist housing

People who are finding it difficult to manage on their own may prefer to move to some sort of specialist housing. In addition to retirement or sheltered housing which has been outlined, there are various types of special housing to suit differing needs.

Extra care retirement housing

Some local councils and housing associations provide sheltered housing that provides extra levels of care. This housing is for people who need personal care services, such as help with dressing or bathing. This accommodation is usually provided in flats and there will normally be a shared lounge and dining rooms where meals are available. Housing in this category is usually run jointly with local authorities and people are placed there after a social services assessment. For more information on such schemes you should contact the Elderly Accommodation Council

Almshouses

Almshouses are run by charitable trusts and in turn provide accommodation for older people. Each charity will have its own rules about the types of people that they house. A few almshouses can provide extra care for vulnerable residents. Residents, as the beneficiaries of charity, do not have the same legal rights as other tenants. The individuals rights will be outlined in a 'letter of appointment' provided by the trustees or the clerk to the trustees. For more information on Almshouses, contacts the Almshouses Association, www.almshouses.org address at the back of this book.

Abbeyfield houses

Abbeyfield provides housing for people in need of sheltered accommodation. Usually this will consist of unfurnished bedsits with shared lounges, dining rooms and a shared garden. The weekly charge will include two meals a day, prepared by a resident housekeeper and also facilities for residents to prepare their own breakfasts and also snacks during the day. Typically, an Abbeyfield resident will be over 75 who is supported by a network of local volunteers. Further details can be obtained from the Abbeyfield Society address at the back of the book.

Housing for those with a disability

Many councils and associations have properties which have been specially designed for people with disabilities. This is referred to as mobility or wheelchair housing. In addition, grants are available for converting existing with disabled access. Councils and housing associations also now build what is known as lifetime homes which are designed to be adapted to peoples needs as they get older.

Living with a relative

If you are thinking of moving in with a relative, or a friend, or if you are thinking of having an older relative live with you, you should always weigh up the pros and the cons of such a move. Some of the things to consider are:

- How well will you get on with the person under the same roof?
- Is there enough space?
- Will a downstairs bedroom be needed?
- Is the housing conveniently situated?
- What are the financial arrangements?
- What are the practical arrangements, such as cooking and washing?
- What would be the implications if you or your relative needed extra care?

You should also speak to your local benefits office about the implications for benefits received when you have made the move.

Moving abroad

Many people dream of leaving the UK and moving to a warmer climate when they have retired. However, the financial climate has changed significantly in the last few years and thorough research is necessary before contemplating such a move. Many people have moved away, particularly to places like Spain, and have returned after a few years, either disillusioned or lonely or having lost money on a property that they have purchased.

It is fairly easy to make enquiries about residency requirements in the various countries. The Foreign and Commonwealth office can provide information and contact details for the relevant consulates or embassies in the various countries. However, before even contemplating such a move, there are various questions that you need to address:

- Can you afford to move to another country? You have to be very clear about your financial situation in retirement. House prices abroad may seem cheap compared to the UK. However, the process of buying can be complicated and some countries, such as Spain, can be problematic. In addition, there has been a collapse in the housing market in Spain due to over development. Caution is advised. You will need to have enough surplus income to live as well so careful planning is needed.
- You will need to think about pension rights and health costs abroad.
- What about possessions? You will need specialist advice about furniture and so on, and the costs of moving.
- Can you take pets? You should always ask a vet's advice first. The Pet Travel Scheme (PETS) allows dogs and cats to re-enter the UK from certain countries without quarantine as long as they meet certain conditions. You can get further information from the Department for Environment, Food and Rural Affairs' PETS Helpline www.defra.gov.uk
- Will you want to find work? You will need professional advice about work permits in the respective countries.

Buying a property abroad

There are property magazines covering homes for sale or rent. Also, property developers are represented at retirement exhibitions. However, a word of caution, you will certainly need professional advice before embarking on a property purchase. It might be useful to buy a book on purchasing a property abroad. You will find case studies of people who have bought successfully and others who have had bad experience. For certain you will need to do your homework well. One useful tip is to ensure that a local agent selling property is working within the rules set by FOPDAC, (The Federation of Overseas Property Developers, Agents and Consultants: www.fopdac.com)

There are also UK firms of solicitors who specialise in the purchase of property abroad. Addresses for such solicitors can typically be found on the Internet.

Repairs and Improvements

One of the most important elements of your home is that of its condition. When you retire or are close to retiring, this presents the ideal opportunity to assess the overall condition of your home and to draw up a condition survey (or have one drawn up) so that you can plan expenditure. It is wise to commence the work as soon as possible after retirement, or before if possible, so that you can still carry out works yourself, without resorting to using building firms. This will save money and mean that you have more control. This chapter also points the way to the various agencies that exist which will give you advice on repairs and maintenance and also funding.

Deciding what needs to be carried out

There are specialist advice agencies, called Home Improvement Agencies (sometimes called Care and Repair or Staying Put) that will give specialist advice to older and vulnerable householders and also to people living in private rented accommodation. They are small scale, not-for-profit organisations, usually managed locally by housing associations, councils or charities. They will usually offer practical help with tasks such as arranging a condition survey, getting estimates from builders (trusted builders) applying for grants or loans and also keeping an eye on the progress of work. They may charge a fee towards their assistance, which is usually included in the grant or loans that you may be in receipt of.

To find out whether there is a home improvement agency in your area, you should contact your local Age UK or the local council housing department or Foundations (the National Co-ordinating Body for Home Improvement Agencies) address at the rear of the book.

If there is no Home Improvement Agency in your area you might want to engage a surveyor to carry one out for you. As these are costly, or can be, you should always ask what the cost will be first. The Chartered Surveyor Voluntary Service exists to help people who would other wise be able to get professional advice. You need to be referred to them by a Citizens Advice Bureau first.

Finding a Builder

If there is no Home Improvement Agency in your area, you should take care, great care, when trying to find a good reliable builder. We have all heard stories of rogue builders who carry out shoddy work and charge over the odds. If you intend to employ a builder, particularly for a larger job, then you should always employ a builder backed by a proper guarantee scheme. The Federation of Master Builders (FMB) offers a MasterBond Warranty: its members must meet certain criteria and adhere to the FMB's Code of Practice. The ten-year insurance backed warranty will add 1.5% to the total cost of a job but is money well spent.

Information on this scheme can be obtained from the FMB website at www.fmb.org.uk. To ensure that you get a good job done, the FMB recommends that you:

- Always ask for references and names of previous clients
- Get estimates from two or three builders
- Ask for the work to be covered by an insurance backed warranty
- Get a written specification and quotation
- Use a contract (the FMB has a plain English contract for small works)
- Agree any staged and final payments before a job
- Avoid dealing in cash

The FMB has played a leading role in the development of the government backed TrustMark scheme, which is a consumer protection initiative for the home repair and improvement sector. A wide range of traders, including plumbers and electricians, are being licensed to become TrustMark registered firms. For more information contact TrustMark address at the rear of this book.

Financial help with repairs and improvements
Sometimes, individuals find themselves in a position where they cannot afford repairs to their homes. There are, however, various forms of assistance at hand. Local authorities have general powers to provide help with repairs and also adaptations to housing. The assistance isn't always cash based, it can also be provided in the form of labour material or advice. The cash element will usually be either grants or loans. Local authorities will have published policies explaining the various forms of

assistance. These can vary from time to time, as many of them are dependant on national legislation and government funding. Below are a few of the types of grants available.

Disabled facilities grant

These grants provide facilities and adaptations to help a disabled person to live as independently and in as much comfort as possible. They are means tested, i.e. dependant on income, with the exception of grants for disabled children. In its assessment, the council will take into account only your income and that of your partner or spouse. The government website www.gov.uk/disabled-facilities-grants outlines all the relevant criteria.

Social services departments provide funding for some minor adaptation works. They may also be able to help with some types of work not covered by the disabled facilities grant.

The Care and Repair England publication also provides useful information about organising and financing building works. You can get a copy by phoning 0115 950 6500 or by downloading it from the website www.careandrepair-england.org.uk.

Adapting your home

You may need to make certain adaptations to your home if you or a member of your family needs them, such as mobility aids, to make it easier to navigate the house. There are other areas that can be helpful, such as the positioning of the furniture. Occupational Therapists can give detailed advice. They can assess a person's mobility and their ability to move around and can provide appropriate advice. You should contact your local social services department and ask for an assessment of needs. You don't have to have a letter from the doctor but this can speed things up. Social services should provide some equipment free if you or a relative is assessed as needing them. All minor adaptations costing less than £1000 must be provided free of charge.

For full information about special equipment and furniture, contact the Disabled Living Foundation www.dlf.org.uk at the address at the rear of the book.

****

Ch. 4

Raising Capital from your Home

Equity release schemes

The main principle behind equity release schemes, which enable you to release cash from your home, is that you are offered a lump sum or an income now but you, or your estate, have to pay back a larger sum to compensate the investors (the Equity release companies). This amounts to a longer-term loan which is paid back later with rolled up interest. If you wish to raise money but do not wish to move home then these schemes could be for you.

Equity release schemes come in two basic forms: lifetime mortgages and home reversion schemes.

Lifetime mortgages

With a lifetime mortgage you borrow against the value of your home but the capital, and usually the interest are repaid only on your death or when you move out. Lifetime mortgages can be taken out jointly with your spouse or partner, in which case the loan does not have to be repaid until the second death. You can use a lifetime mortgage to raise a single large cash sum. If you want an income you can draw out a series of smaller sums or use a single lump sum to buy an investment, such as an annuity. The former is more tax efficient because the income from an annuity is usually taxable.

Types of lifetime mortgages

With the most common form of lifetime loan-a roll up loan-interest is added each month to the amount that you owe. You are charged interest not just on the amount that you originally borrowed, but to the increasing balance as interest is added. The interest can be fixed for the whole life of the loan or can be variable. When your home is eventually sold, the proceeds are used to repay the outstanding loan and what is left over goes to your estate. Different providers set different age limits but you must be at least 55 or 60 with most schemes to be eligible for a lifetime mortgage. In addition, the value of your home, less any debts secured against it must be in the region of £50,000 and upwards. If you have an existing mortgage you will usually be required to pay this off with the loan. The amounts that you can borrow will vary with your age. The maximum for a roll up loan is usually about half the value.

Reversion schemes

With a reversion scheme you sell part, or all, of your home, but retain the right to live there either rent free or for a token rent. When the home is eventually sold, the reversionary company takes a percentage of the sale proceeds, or the whole amount if you sold 100 per cent of your home. This means that the reversion company, as opposed to the estate gets the benefit of any increase in value of your home. A reversion scheme can be taken out singly or jointly, in which case it continues until the second death.

As with lifetime mortgages, reversion schemes can pay you a single lump sum or a series of smaller lump sums. Alternatively, they may be combined with an annuity or other investment to provide you with a regular income. Investment income is usually taxable but lump sums from the sale of your home are not. The

41

money that you get when you take out the loan will be smaller than the value of the part of your home that you sell. This difference represents the return to the reversionary company. A key factor that the reversionary company uses in deciding what it will offer is how long it expects to have to wait before it gets its money back. To qualify for a reversionary scheme you will usually be between 65-70. Your home must be in reasonable condition and worth a minimum amount, typically £75,000.

Alternatives to equity release

One of the most common reasons for considering equity release is to raise extra income for day-to-day living. If this is your main motive, you might want to consider ensuring that the other avenues for raising income have been explored. For example:

- Are you claiming all the state benefits due to you, such as Pension Credit, Council Tax Benefit and Attendance Allowance
- Have you taken steps to trace any lost pensions that you might be claiming?
- Are you exploiting the potential of your home, for example taking in a lodger?
- Are you making sure that you are not overspending?
- Are you paying too much tax?

You cannot normally use equity release to raise a lump sum of below £10,000. If such a sum is needed you might want to consider taking out an interest only mortgage. Unlike a lifetime mortgage you pay interest each month so the amount borrowed does not grow. The main thing with equity release schemes is that you should get good advice, usually independent advice so that you are totally aware of what it is that you are signing up for.

Selling your home

As we all know, the housing market has undergone changes and the value of property, mainly in the South East has increased out of all proportion. However, the wisdom of using your home, or factoring in your home, as a source of income when retirement age is reached, is questionable.

Property prices are just one of the problems if your intention is to sell up to release capital for your retirement. The other main one is that if you are aiming to downsize to a smaller home then the price of this property may not necessarily be that much cheaper than the family home that you are selling. This does depend of course on the nature, size and value of that property. In addition, there are also the other problems associated with relocating, such as getting used to a new area, neighbours and so on.

You should bear in mind as well that there are significant costs associated with selling, moving and buying. This will eat into any equity that you release from your property and should be taken into account. The good news is that stamp duty payable has decreased for most people. Instead of the 'slab' system, i.e. a one off payment you now pay tax on the amount between property bands. For example on a property worth £250,000, given that the first £125,000 is free of tax, you would pay 2% of the remaining £125,000. The system works out cheaper for those who pay more.

The table overleaf will give you an idea of the costs involved.

	COST	EXAMPLE 1. SELLING A HOME FOR £250,000 AND BUYING FOR £150,000	EXAMPLE 2. SELLING A HOME FOR £600,000 AND BUYING FOR £250,000
AS A SELLER			
ESTATE AGENTS FEE	1.5%-2% OF SELLING PRICE	£4375	£10,500
AS A BUYER			
STAMP DUTY LAND TAX	BETWEEN 1-15% OF PROPERTY VALUE	£0	£2500
SURVEYORS FEE	APPROX £500	£500	£500
SEARCH FEES AND LAND REGISTRY FEES	APPROX £500	£500	£500
AS BOTH			
LEGAL COSTS	APPROX £1500	£1500	£1500
REMOVAL COSTS	£600	£600	£600
TOTAL		**£7475**	**£16,100**

Case study
John and Doreen

John and Doreen are selling a £350,000 family home and buying a flat for £200,000. The costs for downsizing are:

- Estate agents fees 1.5% (£5250) Stamp duty land tax 1% of £75,000 = £750
- Survey £500
- Search fees, Land Registry etc £500
- Legal costs on both sales and purchase £1500
- Removal costs £600

Total £9,100. The cash realised from downsizing is £350,000-£200,000-£9,100 = £139,900.

The main advantage of downsizing is that you realise the full value of the home that you are selling (apart from costs). Also, if you are selling your own home the proceeds are tax-free.

****

Ch. 5

Extras because of age

Free bus travel in England for older and disabled people
Eligible older and disabled people are entitled to free off-peak travel on local buses anywhere in England. Off peak is between 9.30am to 11pm Monday to Friday and all day weekends and public holidays.

The England bus pass only covers travel in England. It doesn't give you free bus travel in Wales, Scotland or Northern Ireland.

Free bus travel in Wales, Scotland and Northern Ireland
There are similar schemes in each of the above countries and you need to apply to your respective local authorities.

Who is eligible for an older person's bus pass?
If you live in England, you will be entitled to a bus pass when you reach 'eligible age'. If you were born after 5th April 1950, the age you become eligible is tied to the changes in state pension age for women. This affects both men and women.

Women born after 5th April 1950
If you are a woman born after 5th April 1950, you will become eligible for an older persons bus pass when you reach pensionable age.

Men born after 5th April 1950

If you are a man born after 5th April 1950, you will come eligible when you reach the pensionable age of a woman born on the same day.

If you were born before 6th April 1950

You are eligible for an older person's bus pass from your 60th birthday if you were born before 6th April 1950.

Disabled persons bus pass

You are eligible for a disabled person's bus pass if you live in England and are 'eligible disabled'. This means you:

- are blind or partially sighted
- are profoundly or severely deaf
- are without speech
- have a disability, or have suffered an injury, which has a substantial and long term effect on your ability to walk
- don't have arms or have long-term loss of the use of both arms
- have a learning disability

You are also eligible disabled if your application for a driving licence would be refused under section 92 of the Road Traffic Act 1988 (physical fitness). However, you won't be eligible if you were refused because of persistent misuse of drugs or alcohol.

How to get your bus pass

In the first instance you should contact your local council (whether you live in England, Scotland, Ireland or Wales, who will tell you who issues passes in your area.

Bus passes in London-the Freedom Pass

If you are eligible disabled or of eligible age and you live in Greater London, you can apply for a Freedom Pass. This gives you free travel on the entire Transport for London network. On most services, you can use the pass at any time. You can also use your Freedom Pass England-wide, but only during off-peak times outside of London. If you wish to use your bus pass on coaches then you should ask the coach company about terms and conditions. For more about bus passes for elderly and disabled go to www.gov.uk/apply-for-elderly-person-bus-pass

Passport

If you were born on or before 2nd September 1929, you no longer have to pay for your passport. You can ask for a refund if you are eligible and have applied for a replacement passport since 19th May 2004.

Health

NHS Prescriptions. Once you reach age 60 you qualify for free NHS prescriptions (Currently £8.80 in 2019/20). If you are eligible you simply sign the declaration on the back of the prescription. Scotland and Northern Ireland have phased out charges for prescriptions. Prescriptions are already free for all in Wales.

NHS sight tests. From age 60 you also qualify for free NHS sight tests but you still have to pay for the glasses and lenses, unless your income is low. You can get free sight tests from age 40 if you are considered at risk of developing glaucoma because a close family member has this condition (or any age if you already have sight problems).

Help with bills

Winter fuel payments. This scheme is in force all over the UK and provides a cash sum to every household with one or more people over 60 in the 'qualifying week' which is the week beginning the third Monday in September. You can use the cash in any way you like. However, it is designed specifically to help you cope with Winter fuel bills. The standard payment is normally between £100-£300 depending on your situation. If you want more details concerning this payment you should go to www.directgov.co.uk.

Television licence. Anyone aged 75 or over can apply for a free television licence. It doesn't matter if there are younger people in the household but the licence must be in the name of the person aged 75 or over. If you are already a licence holder you can apply for a cheaper licence for the part year that you turn 75. The licence lasts three years at a time and you should re-apply after three years.

Your home

You can get help with heating and fuel efficiency if you are aged 60 or over. You should go to:
www.gov.uk/browse/benefits/heating.

Repairs and Improvements

One of the most important elements of your home is that of its condition. When you retire or are close to retiring, this presents the ideal opportunity to assess the overall condition of your home and to draw up a condition survey (or have one drawn up) so that you can plan expenditure. It is wise to commence the work as soon as possible after retirement, or before if possible, so that you can still carry out works yourself, without resorting to using building firms. This will save money and mean that you have more control. This chapter also points the way to the various agencies that exist who will give you advice on repairs and maintenance and also funding.

Deciding what needs to be carried out

There are specialist advice agencies, called Home Improvement Agencies (sometimes called Care and Repair or Staying Put) that will give specialist advice to older and vulnerable householders and also to people living in private rented accommodation. They are small scale, no-for-profit organisations, usually managed locally by housing associations, councils or charities. They will usually offer practical help with tasks such as arranging a condition survey, getting estimates from builders (trusted builders) applying for grants or loans and also keeping an eye on the progress of work. They may charge a fee towards their assistance, which is usually included in the grant or loans that you may be in receipt of.

To find out whether there is a home improvement agency in your area, you should contact your local Age UK or the local council housing department or Foundations (the National Co-ordinating Body for Home Improvement Agencies). Address at the rear of the book.

If there is no Home Improvement Agency in your area you might want to engage a surveyor to carry one out for you. As these are costly, or can be, you should always ask what the cost will be first. The Chartered Surveyor Voluntary Service exists to help people who would other wise be able to get professional advice. You need to be referred to them by a Citizens Advice Bureau first.

Finding a Builder

If there is no Home Improvement Agency in your area, you should take care, great care, when trying to find a good reliable builder. We have all heard stories of rogue builders who carry out shoddy work and charge over the odds. If you intend to employ a builder, particularly for a larger job, then you should always employ a builder backed by a proper guarantee scheme. The Federation of Master Builders (FMB) offers a MasterBond Warranty: its members must meet certain criteria and adhere to the FMB's Code of Practice. The ten-year insurance backed warranty will add 1.5% to the total cost of a job but is money well spent.

Information on this scheme can be obtained from the FMB website at www.fmb.org.uk. To ensure that you get a good job done, the FMB recommends that you:

- Always ask for references and names of previous clients
- Get estimates from two or three builders
- Ask for the work to be covered by an insurance backed warranty
- Get a written specification and quotation
- Use a contract (the FMB has a plain English contract for small works)
- Agree any staged and final payments before a job
- Avoid dealing in cash

The FMB has played a leading role in the development of the government backed TrustMark scheme, which is a consumer protection initiative for the home repair and improvement sector.

A wide range of traders, including plumbers and electricians, are being licensed to become TrustMark registered firms. For more information contact TrustMark. Address at the rear of this book.

Financial help with repairs and improvements

Sometimes, individuals find themselves in a position where they cannot afford repairs to their homes. There are, however, various forms of assistance at hand. Local authorities have general powers to provide help with repairs and also adaptations to housing. The assistance isn't always cash based, it can also be provided in the form of labour material or advice. The cash element will usually be either grants or loans. Local authorities will have published policies explaining the various forms of assistance. These can vary from time to time, as many of them are dependant on national legislation and government funding. Below are a few of the types of grants available.

Disabled facilities grant

These grants provide facilities and adaptations to help a disabled person to live as independently and in as much comfort as possible. They are means tested (i.e.) dependant on income, with the exception of grants for disabled children. For more information you should go to www.gov.uk/disabled-facilities-grants

If you receive Pension credit, Income Support or Income based jobseekers allowance, you may be able to get a Community Care Grant or Budgeting Loan from the Social fund to help you with the cost of minor repairs. Social services departments provide funding for some minor adaptation works.

They may also be able to help with some types of work not covered by the disabled facilities grant.

If you want to raise capital from your home to pay for works, the Home Improvement Trust may be able to help. It is a not-for-profit company that has links with a number of commercial lenders who provide older people with low cost loans raised against the value of their home. You can contact Home Improvement Trust direct at the address at the rear of the book.

The Care and Repair England publication also provides useful information about organising and financing building works. You can get a copy by phoning 0115 950 6500 or by downloading it from the website www.careandrepair-england.org.uk.

Adapting your home

You may need to make certain adaptations to your home if you or a member of your family needs them, such as mobility aids, to make it easier to navigate the house. There are other areas that can be helpful, such as the positioning of the furniture. Occupational Therapists can give detailed advice. They can assess a persons mobility and their ability to move around and can provide appropriate advice. You should contact your local social services department and ask for an assessment of needs. You don't have to have a letter from the doctor but this can speed things up. Social services should provide some equipment free if you or a relative is assessed as needing them. All minor adaptations costing less than £1000 must be provided free of charge.

For full information about special equipment and furniture, contact the Disabled Living Foundation at the address at the rear of the book.

****

Ch. 6

Future Care Options

As is well documented over a third of people over 65-74 and over a half over the age of 75 have a long-standing health condition that affects their lives in some way. The ability to carry on living in ones own home really depends a lot on the availability of appropriate care. Quite often this is not readily available, and comes at a cost. Those who are fortunate enough can be cared for by their family.

In 1993, the government introduced policies designed to help more people live independently in their own homes through the expansion of formal support services. This has had the effect of reducing the number of people who need care home support.

However, we are living in an age of an increasing elderly population and there is increase pressure on finances and the ability of government to pay. Whether you are thinking of support in the future for an aging relative or indeed for yourself, there are several main factors that you need to consider and decisions to be made:

- Exactly what form of care might be needed in the future, whether a retirement home or higher level sheltered housing
- Where will the money come from to pay for the care?

For more information about care homes and costs and fees in Scotland go to: www.careinfoscotland.scot/topics/care-homes/paying-care-home-fees/capital-limits.

For Northern Ireland go to:
www.nidirect.gov.uk/articles/your-home-your-assets-and-
your-residential-care.

We need now to examine the various options available.

Care in the home

Most people would rather stay in their own home and receive the appropriate level of support for their needs. Regardless of your own personal financial situation you have the right to approach social services in your local authority area for a needs assessment. Then a manager from the department will visit you in your home (or relative as case may be) and put together a care plan for you.

The whole approach to care in the home and care in residential homes has been redefined by the Care Act 2014, a summary of which is below.

The Care Act 2014

The *Care Act 2014* came into force on 1st April 2015 along with a range of new supporting regulations and a single set of statutory guidance, which, taken together, describe how the Act should be applied in practice. The aim of the change is to simplify and modernise the system, which had become very complex and also to create a new approach to charging. The *Care Act 2014I* actually came into force in two stages, in April 2015 and April 2016. Some of the key changes introduced in 2015 were:

- The promotion of individual well-being as an overarching principle within all the activities of a local authority including: assessment, eligibility, prevention, means testing and care and support planning.

- New national eligibility criterion for both the adult requesting services and their carer(s) leading to rights to services and based around the well-being principle. The previous four local eligibility levels have now become one, set at approximately the previous 'substantial' level. Carers now have an absolute right to have their assessed, eligible, support needs met for the first time; they have a slightly different eligibility criterion to the service user, but are subject to the same means test rules.
- A person-centred, outcomes-focussed, approach to assessing and meeting needs. Local authorities must consider how to meet each person's specific needs rather than simply considering what existing service they will fit into. They must also consider what someone wants/needs to achieve or do and the effect on them of any difficulties they are having.
- The whole system is now administered via personal budgets and based on the principles of the personalisation policy that has been developed over the past few years.
- A 'right to request' service provision for a fee where someone with eligible needs is found to be a self-funder (must pay the whole cost of a service) in the means test. This right does not exist for care home provision.
- New local authority 'market shaping' duties to ensure adequate, diverse, good quality, local service provision.
- The duty to prevent, reduce and delay the need for services and also related duties to integrate care with the NHS where this benefits a service user.
- A lifetime care cost cap (£72,000 in 2019) above which the State will meet the cost of paying a person's eligible

social care needs. The national cap will be reviewed every five years. (keep an eye on this as there have been attempts to change the goal posts and U turns)

- The introduction of care accounts, which will require a local authority to track a person's personal expenditure towards meeting their eligible social care needs, towards the new care cost cap –based on the amount set out in their personal budget. Each account will be adjusted annually in line with the national rise in average earnings. Some local authorities may start to assess for care accounts ahead of the April 2016 start date to avoid capacity issues.

- Independent personal budgets for those people with assessed, eligible, needs but who have capital in excess of the upper threshold and who are meeting the cost of their care and support themselves. This is a choice that will be available to enable payments to be noted in the person's care account.

There are a wide range of support services that can be provided to help you stay in your own home and also to assist your carer if you have one. Services could include: domiciliary (home) carer and personal assistants; meals delivered at home; day center attendance and respite care; live-in care services; rehabilitation services; sheltered accommodation and supported living; shared lives services; other housing options; community support; counseling; direct payment support organisations; information, brokerage and advice services1.

Other forms of assistance could include the provision of specialist disability equipment, adaptations to your home, community alarms and other types of assistive technology.

For more detailed and specific information about the changes and new criteria introduced in the Care Act you should go to www.ageuk.org.uk they have ready prepared fact sheets which will help you to see what you are entitled to.

There are certain fundamental rules that local authorities must abide by. Charges should not reduce the income that a person has left below a set level. If a person is 60 or over, this is the Pension Credit Guarantee credit level plus a buffer which is dependant where you live in the UK, for example 25% in England and 35% in Wales. The assessment should be based only on your income and generally not that of your partner or anyone else. If you feel that you are paying too much for your care services then you have the right to ask the local authority to review your financial assessment.

How the care is paid for

Either the local authority will pay you direct in cash for your services or, if you so desire, you can ask the local authority to arrange and pay for the care. The Government has also introduced a scheme called Individual Budgets, arising out of the Care Act 2014, which are similar to Direct Payment, so you receive a cash sum, but it covers a wide range of services so it includes, for example, help towards a warden in sheltered housing. The aim of cash payments is to put the individual in more control of the services that they buy. Obviously, this may not be suited to everyone and some people will be more reliant on the local authority to provide and pay for services.

Other benefits available

There are other benefits available such as personal independence payment (replacing Disability Living allowance for those up to age 64) or if you are over 65 Attendance Allowance.

These benefits are tax-free and are not means tested. If you are a carer, you will also have the right to a free needs assessment to pay for extra levels of need.

The care plan devised by the local authority might for example recommend that someone be paid for sitting with a relative whilst you have a few hours off, or respite care (where the disabled person moves temporarily into a care home). You will be expected to pay for these services unless your income and savings are low .

Retirement housing

Retirement housing is known by a number of different names that usually reflects the level of care needed, for example sheltered housing, warden assisted housing or warden controlled housing. This is designed for people over 60 (sometimes can be 55). Usually, it is a scheme that comprises a number of flats and maybe a few bungalows with communal areas for residents, such as lounge and gardens and in some cases a kitchen for the provision of communal meals. There is also usually a laundry area and an emergency call system plus a warden if included in the overall scheme cost.

Some schemes are private, people buy a lease, known as leasehold schemes for the elderly. Sheltered housing to rent is normally provided by local authorities and, more usually now, housing associations. To qualify for these schemes you have to prove that you are in need and cannot afford to buy. You may qualify for Housing Benefit.

The main cost associated with retirement housing, whether rented or owned, is the service charge. As an ex-care home manager myself, I have long experience of the difficulties that surround service charges.

The service charge covers the cost of wardens, communal areas, emergency call system and gardening. Many other areas are included. If you are on a low income then you might be eligible for housing benefit for some of the services.

Ordinary sheltered housing does not include care services, this has to be arranged with your local authority. However, as discussed, sheltered housing can be more intensive and the levels of charges will reflect this. For example do you, or a relative envisage needing intensive care of a kind provided by category one sheltered housing or will you need a lesser degree of care?

Moving to a care home

If you move to a care home to receive personal care you may have to pay some or all of the fees yourself, depending on your income. If your main aim is health care, the NHS should pay. This is called NHS continuing care. In some circumstances, you may receive care at home either to avoid admission to hospital or to enable you to leave hospital early. In this case, you are entitled to free care-called intermediate care-which may include a mix of health and social care. The social care element should be free for a maximum of six weeks.

If your primary reason for moving to a care home is for help with personal care such as getting up, going to bed, bathing and so on, in general you are expected to pay for the fees yourself unless your income and savings are low. In that case, the local authority will carry out a financial assessment to determine whether you should pay anything at all. This assessment is in line with the capital limits which can be obtained from your local authority.

Even if your main need is personal care, you may require some nursing care as well and this is provided free, up to set limits depending where you live in the UK and, in England, on the extent of the nursing care that you need.

The Government pays these sums direct to your care provider. If you are paying for your care home fees yourself, you are likely to qualify for Attendance Allowance. If the NHS or local authority is paying for some or all of the fees, you will not be able to get Attendance Allowance as well.

As described above, the Care Act 2014 has affected the way in which home care and care home funding is allocated and you should contact Age UK to find out more.

Assessing your finances

Whether or not you can get state funding depends in part on how much capital you have (means testing). Capital includes savings and investments but can also include your house, However, if your partner (married or not), an elderly or disabled relative or a child under 16 still lives there, the value of your home is disregarded. The local authority also has the discretion to ignore your home, if, for example, you carer will carry on living there.

How will my capital be treated in the means test?

You capital is the phrase used to describe the total amount of your savings, any property you own and any shares you might have. It does not include your pension and benefits you might be getting.

For England, Wales and Northern Ireland the below limits are applicable ion 2019.

For Scotland go to www.careinfoscotland.scot/topics/care-homes/paying-care-home-fees/capital-limits.

Amount of your capital	How it will be treated
Over £23,250	You must pay full fees (self-funding)
Between £14,250 and £23,250	The local authority will assume that this generates an income and this will be taken into account for your care home fee contributions.
Less than £14,250	This will be ignored and won't be included in the means test

If you are a couple, the local authority is not allowed to base the financial assessment on your joint resources. It must consider only the capital and income that belongs to you. If you are holding assets on behalf of someone else you must prove that they are not your assets or the local authority will treat them as your assets. You can be treated as still owning capital if you are deemed to have deliberately deprived yourself of it. This could be the case if you have given away assets to other family members in advance of applying for a care assessment. Spouses and civil partners are in law liable to support each other and can be asked to contribute towards fees, but the local authority should not do this if it would cause financial hardship. The local authority cannot ask an unmarried partner or other family member to contribute.

How much will I have to pay?

After the means test the local authority should give you a written record of their decision of what you will have to pay and what they will pay, and how they calculated it. You should not be left with less than £24.90 a week after any contribution to your fees. This is known as your Personal Expenses Allowance.

What if I run out of money?

If you are paying fees yourself (called self-funding) and your capital goes down to less than £23,250, the local authority may assist with funding. You should request an assessment a few months before that happens. They should arrange one as soon as possible so you don't have to use up your capital below that amount.

Planning ahead for care

If you think that you will need care for a long time, taking out a long-term care product could work out cheaper than the fees. Planning ahead is very difficult and there is no real way to know what your needs will be. There are a few providers of long-term care products and these tend to be expensive. One obvious route is to take out some form of insurance. In the UK, there is just one provider of long-term care insurance. It targets healthy individuals aged 50-70 years. With high premiums (for example around £100 per month for a policy that would pay out a flat rate of £1000 a month it is easy to see why the take up of this insurance is limited.

A handful of providers offer what is known as impaired life annuities that you buy at the point when you need care. You pay a lump sum and in return get an income that pays all or a substantial part of your care costs. The income is tax-free provided that it is paid direct to the provider. The amount that you pay for the annuity will depend on the monthly payments that you need and also the annuity providers assessment of how long that it will have to pay out.

Ch. 7

Income Tax Generally-How it Affects You

Income Tax

Regardless of whether we are employed, retired or self-employed, we all have to accept the fact that HMRC are going to take a percentage of our income in the form of income tax and there is nothing we can do to avoid it.

The retired, employed and self-employed are treated in slightly different ways and therefore we shall look at each individually, once we have assessed the structure of income tax. You should check your current tax allowances with HM Revenue and Customs as they are subject to annual change. For more information about tax and state and other pensions see chapter 9 onwards

Personal allowance

Most people are allowed to receive a certain amount of income before tax is payable. This is known as the basic personal allowance. In 2019-20 allowances are:

Band	Taxable income	Tax rate
Personal Allowance	Up to £12,500	0%
Basic rate	£12,501 to £50,000	20%
Higher rate	£50,001 to £150,000	40%
Additional rate	over £150,000	45%

You don't get a Personal Allowance on taxable income over £125,000.

Income above £100,000

If your income is above £100,000, basic personal allowance is further reduced by £1 for each £2 earned over the £100,000 limit, irrespective of age.

Blind person's allowance

You may also be entitled to an additional allowance if you or your spouse or registered civil partner are blind or have severely impaired sight.

This is another full relief allowance as it is treated in the same way as the personal allowance, so increases the amount of income you can receive before you start to pay tax. In 2019-20 this allowance is £2,450.

In England and Wales

If you live in England or Wales, you will need to be certified as blind and appear on a local authority register of blind people to claim this allowance.

In Scotland and Northern Ireland

If you have not been certified as blind and live in Scotland or Northern Ireland you will qualify for the allowance if your eyesight is so bad that you are unable to perform any work where your eyesight is essential.

Unused balance

If your income is not enough to make use of the allowance, any unused balance can be transferred to your spouse or registered civil partner. Married couples get certain tax breaks

Married couple's allowance

You only qualify for this allowance if you or your husband, wife or registered civil partner were born before 6 April 1935. Unlike the personal allowance, the married couple's allowance is not an amount you can earn before you start paying tax. Instead, it's a restricted relief allowance, which means the tax you pay is reduced by deducting 10% of the allowance from your final tax bill.

Marriage transferable tax allowance

Additionally, from April 2019, married couples born after 1935 will be able to transfer up to £1,250 of unused personal allowance (Marriage transferable tax allowance).

Claiming maintenance relief

You can claim this relief for certain maintenance payments you make if you or your ex-spouse or registered civil partner were born before 6 April 1935 and you pay the maintenance under a legally binding agreement. It works in a similar way to the married couple's allowance. Your tax bill will be reduced by 10% of the maintenance relief allowance or the amount you pay in maintenance, if that amount is lower.

The Employed

If you are employed your tax affairs are conducted on the fiscal year or financial year which is 6th April to 5th April the following year.   You are taxed on what is known as Schedule E (Pay As You Earn) which means that both tax and national insurance will be deducted by your employer before you receive your salary. You therefore receive your salary net of tax. This is without doubt the simplest way to conduct your tax affairs as there is very little further communication you need to have, if any, with your tax office.

At the end of the financial year you will receive a P60 which is a statement of your full year's earnings and it will contain details of how much tax and national insurance you have paid as well as pension contributions if you are in an occupational pension scheme.

You should always keep your P60 in a safe place as it often requested by banks and building societies for mortgage or loan purposes.

If you work for a large employer you may receive fringe benefits such as a company car, mortgage subsidy, or private medical insurance. These are very worthwhile benefits but you must remember they are also taxable benefits which will mean that your personal allowance will reduce to account for the real value of these benefits. If you have such benefits but notice your tax code hasn't changed then it is your responsibility to inform your tax office, as failure to do so may mean that in future years they could claim payment for undisclosed benefits.

Not all benefits are taxable, however, and the most attractive one is obviously a company pension scheme. In recent years a great deal of companies have moved towards Performance Related Pay. When you leave employment you will be provided with a P45 which is similar to a P60 but is for the benefit of your new employer to use in order to calculate your earnings to date and therefore make the necessary stoppages in your salary. It is always worthwhile taking a copy of your P45 for your own reference.

The self-employed

If you are self employed your own tax year can be any period of 12 months you want. In the eyes of the Inland Revenue you will be taxed on what is known as Schedule D and pay Class 2 National Insurance contributions.

Being self employed means that the money you receive for the services you provide will be gross and therefore no tax will have been deducted.

It is advisable that you keep an accurate record of all the money you receive and receipts for any money you spend in connection with your business activities. At the beginning of April you would normally receive a tax return form which explores all the potential sources of income you may have. This must be duly signed and returned within a month.

A large percentage of the self employed use the services of an accountant, as they best know the ways in which your tax liability can be reduced and their services certainly make it easier if you are self-employed and are hoping to take out a mortgage.

HM Revenue and Customs will negotiate with you or your accountant once they have details of your year's earnings and business expenses. Once the expenses have been taken from the gross figure this will leave your net income and therefore the amount upon which you will be expected to pay tax.

Your tax liability is normally paid in 2 installments, the first on 1st January and the second on the 1st July. The Inland Revenue, however, do not wait for your accounts to be completed and in most cases you will be expected to make installments based on assessments of your expected income and once your accounts are finalised you will then be informed of any over or under payment.

Tax and pensions

You pay tax if your total annual income adds up to more than your Personal Allowance. Your total income could include:

- the State Pension you get (either the basic State Pension or the new State Pension)
- Additional State Pension
- a private pension (workplace or personal) - you can take some of this tax-free
- earnings from employment or self-employment
- any taxable benefits you get
- any other income, such as money from investments, property or savings

You may have to pay Income Tax at a higher rate if you take a large amount from a private pension. You may also owe extra tax at the end of the tax year.

If your private pensions total more than £1 million

You usually pay a tax charge if the total value of your private pensions is more than £1 million. Your pension provider will take off the charge before you get your payment.

Tax if someone inherits your pension

Other rules apply if someone inherits your State pension or your private pension.

You won't usually pay any tax if your total annual income adds up to less than your Personal Allowance.

Lump sums from your pension

You can usually take up to 25% of the amount built up in any pension as a tax-free lump sum. The tax-free lump sum doesn't affect your Personal Allowance. Tax is taken off the remaining amount before you get it.

Example:

Your whole pension is worth £60,000. You take £15,000 tax-free. Your pension provider takes tax off the remaining £45,000. When you can take your pension depends on your pension's rules. It's usually 55 at the earliest. You might have to pay Income Tax at a higher rate if you take a large amount from your pension. You could also owe extra tax at the end of the tax year.

How you can take your pension
A pension worth up to £10,000

You can usually take any pension worth up to £10,000 in one go. This is called a 'small pot' lump sum. If you take this option, 25% is tax-free.

You can usually get:

- up to 3 small pot lump sums from different personal pensions
- unlimited small pot lump sums from different workplace pensions

A pension worth up to £30,000 that includes a defined benefit pension

If you have £30,000 or less in all of your private pensions, you can usually take everything you have in your defined benefit pension as a 'trivial commutation' lump sum. If you take this option, 25% is tax-free. If this lump sum is paid from more than one pension, you must:

- have your savings in each scheme valued by the provider on the same day, no more than 3 months before you get the first payment
- get all payments within 12 months of the first payment

If you take payments from a pension before taking the rest as a lump sum, you pay tax on the whole lump sum.

Cash from a defined contribution pension

Check with your provider about how you can take money from a defined contribution pension. You can take:

- all the money built up in your pension as cash - up to 25% is tax-free
- smaller cash sums from your pension - up to 25% of each sum is tax-free

You may have to pay a tax charge on money you put into your pension after you withdraw cash.

If your life expectancy is less than a year

You may be able to take all the money in your pension as a tax-free lump sum, if all of the following apply:

- you're expected to live less than a year because of serious illness

- you're under 75
- you don't have more than the lifetime allowance of £1 million in pension savings

If you're over 75 you'll pay Income Tax on the lump sum. Check with your pension provider. Some pension funds will keep at least 50% of your pension for your spouse or civil partner.

Capital Gains Tax

If you have successfully bought and sold investments, antiques and property etc., you may find that you would be liable for capital gains tax. Everyone is allowed to make a profit on opportunities that they fund with their own capital. There is, however, a limit, which you should check with HMRC, and any profit/gain that exceeds that figure would be liable for capital gains tax at the individual's marginal rate.

Tax on dividends from April 2016

You may get a dividend payment if you own shares in a company. In April 2018/19, the first £2,000 is tax free.

Above this allowance the tax you pay depends on which Income Tax band you're in. Add your income from dividends to your other taxable income when working this out. You may pay tax at more than one rate.

Tax band	Tax rate on dividends over £2,000
Basic rate	7.5%
Higher rate	32.5%
Additional rate	38.1%

Inheritance Tax

The subject of death is one which is rarely discussed openly and inheritance tax is thought to be an issue that is largely limited to the wealthy. This however, is a misconception, as inheritance tax will affect more people now than ever before. In order to establish whether you are going to have an inheritance tax bill, you must assess the total value of the estate left by the deceased. This would include all assets and any gifts made within the preceding seven years. If the total figure exceeds £325.000 (2019-20) there will be a liability on the surplus of 40%. If the estate totals less than £325,000 there will be no liability. You should check these limits with HMRC as they are subject to change. It now becomes clear that if you have been able to build a reasonable amount of savings, paid off your mortgage and may have received a pension lump sum and an inheritance yourself, you could be bordering on the £325,000 limit and your estate would be liable for inheritance tax. You should not restrict your own lifestyle in order to reduce your beneficiaries' tax bill but if you can afford it there are various options and exemptions that could substantially reduce the future liability.

Exemptions

1. There is no inheritance tax between husband and wife.
2. To a U.K charity.
3. Gifts that total £3,000 a year.
4. £250 gifts made to anyone and however many people you like. This cannot be given to the same people as the £3,000.
5. Wedding presents, £5,000 from a parent, £2,500 from a grandparent, £1,000 from friend or family.
6. Part of a divorce settlement.

7. To support female parent-in-law if she is divorced, widowed or separated.

8. Selected agricultural land or business assets and unquoted shares.

Gifts made seven years before death

Any gifts that the deceased made in the last 7 years of his or her life will be liable to inheritance tax on a sliding scale and the value of the gift will also form part of the estate. In order to reduce the liability you could write any life insurance policies you have under trust and should you die, the benefits of your policies would not form part of your estate, but be payable to your spouse or children, therefore avoiding possible inheritance tax. For more detailed advice on taxation you should go to the HMRC website at www. hmrc.gov.uk

****

Ch. 8

Making a Will

It is often said that the toughest job in sales is to get people to buy fire extinguishers: no one wants to think that they and their family could be caught in a fire which could kill or injure. The same thinking seems to apply to making a will: most people in Britain have not made a will- something which their families could well come to regret.

There are two sorts of people for whom making a will is not just a good idea, but essential: Anyone who is reasonably well off or whose affairs are at all complicated, and anyone who is in a partnership. Unmarried partners (or outside a civil arrangement) cannot inherit from each other unless there is a will: your partner could end up with nothing when you die, unless they can show that they were financially dependent.

There is no such thing in England as a 'common-law marriage.'

The State moves in

When anyone dies without making a will, the law, i.e. the state, takes over. In the extreme case, where you die single and have no other surviving relatives, all your estate could end up with the Crown. And the law is not at all generous to your spouse: if you have no children, your widow or widower is entitled to the first £200,000 of assets and 50% of what remains - the rest ending up with brothers and sisters, if you have any, or with relatives you cannot remember. If there are children, the widow/widower will get £125,000, plus personal assets and income from 50% of the rest; the children will get 50% when they reach age 18 and the other 50% when the surviving parents dies. If you aim to save inheritance tax, you need to make a will. For 2017-18 the 'nil rate band' is fixed at £325,000 which means that no tax is due below that level, and anything more is taxed at 40%.

How to make a will

So how do you make a will? You can draw up your own using a will-making kit which you can buy from a big stationer or download from the net. That represents the most cost-effective choice and it could work if your affairs are reasonably straightforward. But if you think that your will could be disputed, i.e. subject to legal challenge, then you need to go to a solicitor. That will be a few hundred pounds well spent and you may qualify for legal aid on financial grounds or because of age: you could ask Citizens Advice. You will probably know a solicitor or have employed one in a recent property deal. You will talk to friends or you can contact the Law Society for a list of solicitors near where you live.

Put yourself on paper

Before you go to your solicitor, there are two important things you need to do. Firstly, you need to put yourself on paper - everything you own that is of significant size, including cars, jewellery, property, home contents, bank accounts, shares and life insurance. At the same time, you put down all that you owe, such as mortgage, overdraft and credit card debts. You need to give precise details of the beneficiaries and be very specific about what you are leaving them.

The second thing you need to do is choose an executor, one or two people whose job is to ensure that your wishes are carried out. Your first thought may be someone younger than you (you will need their agreement to act) but there is no guarantee that they will outlive you. If no executor has been designated, the state will appoint a solicitor for you - for a fee. If you go to a solicitor, think about a formula, e.g. a partner appointed by whoever is senior partner of the firm at the time. The executors will need to know where your will is kept, with your solicitor or in your bank.

Time to revisit?

You have made your will, but you should resolve to look at it again, say every five years: people change, as do assets and liabilities. It is a good basic rule to revisit your will when a new child arrives or when you move house. Outside events can change a will: if you were single when you drew up your will, it may become invalid if you get married. But divorce or separation do not make a will invalid, so you might want to make changes. If you just want to make minor alterations, you can add supplementary changes known as codicils. These are added separately and all alterations have to be properly witnessed. If the alterations are significant, you will need to make a new will which will revoke any other wills you have made.

The case for making a will is essentially simple: as Benjamin Franklin said, death and taxes are certain, and making a will means that your family will not have to spend time and energy sorting out a complicated financial and legal set-up. But when you look beyond middle age you have to assess probabilities - you may be out of the country when your signature is needed, you may get ill or you may be injured. We are now talking power of attorney.

Power of attorney

You probably gave your solicitor a power of attorney when you sold your flat; you may have given a power of attorney to your partner when you had to go on an overseas business trip but wanted to buy some shares in the UK. A power of attorney simply gives a person the power to act for somebody else in their financial affairs or in health and personal welfare. (Rules in Scotland are different). The power of attorney you gave your solicitor was probably an ordinary power of attorney, created for a set period of time and for a specific piece of business. That all seems very practical, you may think, but why should you give anyone a power of attorney? The short answer is that if you are away or fall ill, you will need someone to look after your affairs - and that requires a power of attorney. (If this happens and you had not given a power of attorney, your friends and relatives would have to go to court, which would take time and cost money)

Ending the power

When you have given a power of attorney, there are two ways in which it can be ended. You can end it yourself by using a deed of revocation or it will end automatically if you, the donor, lose 'mental capacity.' This is where problems can arise. Suppose you gave your partner an ordinary power of attorney to handle your bank account while you go on your overseas business trip; you are mugged while on your trip and lie unconscious in hospital. Your power of attorney is ended because you are mentally out of action; for the same reason you cannot give a new power of attorney. Your partner cannot legally access your bank account or have any involvement in your affairs: catch 22? Until last year, the answer to this puzzle was to create an Enduring Power of Attorney. Under an EPA when you were mugged on your overseas trip, your partner and/or solicitor would register with the court and they could then act on your behalf. New EPAs cannot be created since October 2007.

New lasting powers

EPA's have been replaced by Lasting Powers of Attorney which have separate sections for personal welfare and for property and affairs. Each of these has to be registered separately and the LP A can only be used - similar to an EPA - once it has been registered with the Office of the Public Guardian. If you want to change your mind, you can cancel all the different Powers of Attorney, so long as you are still mentally capable. This may all sound elaborate but it represents the only answer to the situation where you cannot manage your affairs because of accident, illness, age or whatever - but someone needs to do so.

The need for a power of attorney is now that much greater because banks and financial institutions are more aware of their legal responsibilities. Formerly, a friendly bank manager might have been prepared to help your partner sort out what needed to be done while you were out of action. Now, your friendly bank manager is more likely to stick to the legal rules, if only to protect himself and his employer.

You as attorney

One of your colleagues may ask you to be his attorney; if you agree, make sure that a firm of solicitors are also involved. You will have some costs - such as when you register the power of attorney - and there are strict rules, for keeping money and property separate and for keeping accounts of any dealings for the person who gave you the power. When you register, you are obliged to tell your colleague's relatives who are free to object. This is not a job for a layman acting all by himself

Chapter 9

Pensions and Planning for the Future

Planning for the future

The main principle with all pension provision is that the sooner you start saving money in a pension plan the more you will have at retirement. The later that you leave it the less you will have or the more expensive that it will be to create a fund adequate enough for your needs.

In order to gauge your retirement needs, you will need to have a clear idea of your lifestyle, or potential lifestyle in retirement. This is not something that you can plan, or want to plan, at a younger age but the main factor is that the more that you have the easier life will be. There are two main factors which currently underpin retirement:

- Improved health and longevity-we are living longer and we have better health so therefore we are more active
- People are better off-improved state and company pensions

Sources of pension and other retirement income

Government statistics indicate that there is a huge gap between the poorest and richest pensioners in the United Kingdom. No surprise there. The difference between the richest fifth of single pensioners and the poorest fifth is about £400 per week. The poorest fifth of pensioners in the UK are reliant mainly on state benefits whilst the wealthier groups have occupational incomes and also personal investment incomes.

The outline below indicates sources of pension and also the disparity between the richest and poorest socio-economic groups:

The Pensioners Income Series

The Pensioners' Incomes (PI) Series, produced by the Government, contains estimates of the levels, sources and distribution of pensioners' incomes. It also examines the position of pensioners within the income distribution of the population as a whole.

Pensioners Income Series 2016/2017

Pensioners have seen an increase in their average weekly incomes over the past decade

- After the deduction of direct taxes, other payments such as pension contributions and housing costs, the average income of all pensioners in 2016/17 was £307 per week. This is a statistically significant increase from 2006/07 when it was £260. This change reflects increases in occupational pension, earnings and benefits.
- In 2016/17 the average income for pensioner couples was £452 per week. This was more than twice that of single pensioners, who had an average income of £214 per week. This difference is statistically significant.
- Income flattened slightly around 2009/10 after the financial crisis which began in 2008.

One fifth of pensioner couples' income was from earnings

- Pensioners receive income from a range of different sources and changes in the composition of these sources reflect important underlying economic factors.
- In 2016/17, benefit income was the largest component of total gross income for pensioner couples and single pensioners. This percentage was 56 per cent for single pensioners, for pensioner couples this was 36 per cent.
- Income from occupational pension was 31 per cent of total gross income for pensioner couples and 28 per cent for single pensioners.
- Income from earnings made up seven per cent of total income for single

---

pensioners. For pensioner couples, one fifth of total income was from earnings. A pensioner couple can sometimes include one adult below SPa who may be working.

■ Pensioner couples where one is over SPa and one is under had a weekly average income from earnings of £439. Average income from earnings was £291 per week for pensioner couples where they were both over SPa.

Older pensioners had lower incomes than younger pensioners

■ Both recently retired pensioners and pensioners where the head was under 75 had higher average incomes than those where the head was 75 or over. These results were statistically significant.

■ In 2016/17, their average incomes were £380, £361 and £265 per week, respectively. Recently retired pensioners are also included in the 'Under 75' age group.

■ In 2016/17 the majority of pensioners where the head is 75 or over were single pensioners (64 per cent). On average single pensioners have lower incomes. More information about single pensioners' incomes is discussed on the previous page.

Almost one third of the total income for pensioners was from occupational pensions

■ Earnings accounted for 22 per cent of total gross income for recently retired pensioners and pensioners where the head was under 75. For pensioners where the head was aged 75 or over, this was four per cent. Older pensioners are less likely to be in work and hence receive a smaller amount from earnings.

■ Benefit income made up more than half of total gross income for pensioners where the head was aged 75 or over. For recently retired pensioners and pensioners where the head was under 75, benefit income made up 34 per cent and 36 per cent of total gross income respectively.

■ Occupational pension income was 29 per cent of total gross income for recently retired pensioners and pensioners where the head was under 75. This was 31 per cent for pensioners where the head was aged 75 or over.

■ Incomes from personal pension and investment were similar percentages of total gross income for all groups.

■ In 2016/17 53 per cent of recently retired pensioners received more than 50 per cent of their gross income from private sources.

Single men had a higher income than single women

■ Single male pensioners had higher average incomes than single female pensioners. In 2016/17, single men had an average weekly income of £233 and single women had an average weekly income of £206. This difference is statistically significant.

■ The difference was greatest among pensioners aged over 75. Single men in this age group had an average weekly income of £246 per week compared to women who had an average weekly income of £204 per week. This difference is statistically significant.

■ In 2016/17 the majority of single female pensioners were aged 75 and over (58 per cent). As seen on page four, older pensioners on average have lower incomes.

Over half of the total income for single women pensioners was from benefit income

■ The difference in incomes reflects differences in the components that make up an individual's total gross income.

■ Benefit income made up 61 per cent of total gross income for single women. For single men, this value was 48 per cent.

■ Thirty-one per cent of total gross income for single men was from occupational pension. For single women, this was 26 per cent.

■ Income from earnings made up nine per cent of total gross income for single men. For single women, this was six per cent.

Regional differences

Pensioner incomes differed between regions and countries.

When looking at regional incomes we take the average weekly income (AHC) for each region over the three year period 2014/15 to 2016/17, adjusted to 2016/17 prices.

■ For pensioner couples, the majority of regions have average weekly incomes below the UK average.

■ The UK average weekly income over this three year period was £447 for pensioner couples.

■ On average, pensioner couple incomes were lowest in Wales, where income was 12 per cent below the UK average. In comparison, pensioner couples in the South East had the highest average incomes, 12 per cent higher than the UK average. This difference is statistically significant.

■ Pensioner couples in Scotland average income was the same as the UK average.

Sources of pensioner incomes -Percentage of pensioners receiving income from private pensions has increased

- Nearly all pensioners (97 per cent) were in receipt of the State Pension in 2016/17. This has increased from 1996/97, where 94 per cent of all pensioners were in receipt of State Pension. This result is statistically significant.

- Income-related benefits were received by 24 per cent of all pensioners in 2016/17. The percentage of pensioners in receipt has decreased from 37 per cent in 1996/97; this is statistically significant. This reflects for example increases in other sources of income, particularly income from State Pension and Private Pension, reducing eligibility to Income related benefits for pensioners.

- Twenty-one per cent of pensioners were in receipt of disability benefits in 2016/17; this has increased by three percentage points from 1996/97. This increase is statistically significant.

- Over the past 20 years, there has been an increase of nine percentage points in the percentage of pensioners receiving income from private pensions – from 62 per cent to 71 per cent; this is statistically significant.

- There has been an increase of three percentage points in the percentage of pensioners with income from occupational pensions – from 59 per cent in 1996/97 to 62 per cent in 2016/17.

- Personal pensions provide income to a smaller group of pensioners than occupational pensions. In 2016/17, 19 per cent of pensioners were in receipt of income from personal pensions, compared with four per cent in 1996/97. This increase is statistically significant. Personal pensions in their current form were introduced in 1988.

- Investment income was received by 62 per cent of all pensioners in 2016/17. The percentage of pensioners in receipt has decreased over the past 20 years, from 71 per cent in 1996/97. This difference is statistically significant. The decrease between 2006/07 and 2016/17 was predominantly in 2010/11 to 2012/13. This period follows the financial crisis, which started in 2008.

- Overall 17 per cent of pensioners were in receipt of earnings in 2016/17, compared to 11 percent in 1996/97. This is a statistically significant increase. This includes pensioner couples where one partner was under SPa.

SUMMARY OF IMPORTANT FACTS

State Pension

Almost all pensioners (97 per cent) received income from State Pension, with an average income of £167. Twenty per cent of those in receipt had an income of over £250.

Income-related benefits

Twenty-four per cent of pensioners were in receipt of income-related benefits. Of those in receipt the average income was £77.

Disability benefits

Twenty-one per cent of pensioners were in receipt of disability benefits and the average income was £81. Some benefits have set rates, which may explain peaks in the distribution. For example, Attendance Allowance has a lower rate of £55.10 and a higher rate of £82.30.

Private pension

Seventy-one per cent of pensioners received income from a private pension with an average amount of £158. Fourteen per cent of those in receipt had an income of over £500.

.

Occupational pension

Over half of all pensioners (62 per cent) were in receipt of an occupational pension and the average amount was £161. Fourteen per cent of those in receipt had an occupational pension income of over £500.

.

Personal pension

Nineteen per cent of pensioners had income from a personal pension with an average of £51. Twenty-three per cent of pensioners in receipt had a personal pension income of less than £20.

.

Investments

Sixty-two per cent of pensioners were in receipt of investment income with an average income of £6. Six per cent of pensioners had a weekly income of over £250.

.

Earnings

Seventeen per cent of pensioners were in receipt of earnings with an average income of £322. Fifteen per cent of pensioners had an income of over £1,000 per week.

Amongst other things, the above illustrates that those in the poorest and wealthiest bands have a wide gap in income, in particular in the areas of earnings and investments. The richest have managed to ensure that there is enough money in the pot to cater for retirement. Those in the lower income bands rely heavily on state pensions and other benefits. The Pensioners Income Series measures those within the bottom, middle and top fifth of the population.

For more information on the Pensioner Income Series you should go to www.gov.uk/government/collection/pensioners-income-series-statistics-july-2016/17. There is a whole array of comparisons and general information, most of it quite interesting.

Ch. 10

How Much Income is needed in Retirement-Planning Ahead

When attempting to forecast for future pension needs, there are a number of factors which need to be taken into account: These are:

- Your income needs in retirement and how much of that income you can expect to derive from state pensions
- How much pension that any savings you have will produce
- How long you have to save for
- Projected inflation

Income needs in retirement

This is very much a personal decision and will be influenced by a number of factors, such as ongoing housing costs, care costs, projected lifestyle etc. The main factor is that you have enough to live on comfortably. In retirement you will probably take more holidays and want to enjoy your free time. This costs money so your future planning should take into account all your projected needs and costs. When calculating future needs, all sources of income should be taken into account.

What period to save over

The obvious fact is that, the longer period that you save over the more you will build up and hence the more that you will have in retirement. As time goes on savings are compounded and the value of the pot goes up. One thing is for certain and that is if you leave it too late then you will have to put away a large slice of your income to produce a decent pension. If you plan to retire at an early age then you will need to save more to produce the same benefits.

Inflation

As prices rise, so your money buys you less. This is the main effect of inflation and to maintain the same level of spending power you will need to save more as time goes on. Many forms of retirement plans will include a calculation for inflation. Currently, inflation is at 2.7% (January 2019) expected to fall to 2.1% by the third quarter. However, history shows that the effects of inflation can be corrosive, having risen above 25% per annum in the past. Hopefully, this is now under control

For most people, retirement is a substantial part of life, probably lasting a couple of decades or more. It follows that ensuring your financial security in retirement requires some forward planning. Developing a plan calls for a general review of your current finances and careful consideration of how you can build up your savings to generate the retirement income that you need.

There are five distinct stages to planning your retirement which are summarised below.

Stage 1-this involves checking first that other aspects of your basic finances are in good shape. Planning for retirement generally means locking away your money for a long time. Once invested it is usually impossible to get pension savings back early, even in an emergency. It is therefore essential that you have other more accessible savings available for emergencies and that you do not have any problem debts that could tip you into a financial crisis. You must then weigh up saving for retirement against other goals that are more pressing, such as making sure that your household would be financially secure if you were unable to work because of illness or the main breadwinner dies.

Stage 2-You need to decide how much income you might need when you retire. There is a table overleaf which might help you in calculating this.

Stage 3- Check how much pension that you have built up so far.

Stage 4-Compare your amount from stage 3 with your target income from stage 2.

Stage 5-Review your progress once a year and/or if your circumstances change.

It is a fact that many people need far less in retirement than when actively working. The expenses that exist when working, such as mortgage payments, children and work related expenses do not exist when retired. The average household between 30-49 spends £473 per week and £416 between 50-64. This drops to £263 per week between 65 to 74 and even lower in later retirement (Expenditure and Food Survey).

However, as might be expected, expenditure on health care increases correspondingly with age. Whilst the state may help with some costs the individual still has to bear a high proportion of expenditure on health related items. When calculating how much money you will need in retirement, it is useful to use a table in order to list your anticipated expenses as follows

Everyday needs

Item	Annual Total
Food and other	
Leisure (newspapers etc)	
Pets	
Clothes	
Other household items	
Gardening	
General expenses	

Home expenses

Mortgage/rent	
Service charges/repairs	
Insurance	
Council tax	
Water and other utilities	
Telephone	
TV licence other charges (satellite)	
Other expenses (home help)	

Leisure and general entertainment

Hobbies	
Eating out	
Cinema/theatre	
Holidays	

Other luxuries (smoking/drinking	

Transport

Car expenses	
Car hire	
Petrol etc	
Bus/train fares	

Health

Dental charges	
Optical expenses	
Medical insurance	
Care insurance	
Other health related expenses	

Anniversaries/birthdays etc

Children/grandchildren	
Relatives other than children	
Christmas	
Charitable donations	
Other expenses	

Savings and loans

General savings	
Saving for later retirement	
Other savings	
Loan repayments	

Other

The above should give you an idea of the amounts that you will need per annum to live well. Obviously, you should plan for a monthly income that will meet those needs. You should also take account of income tax on your retirement incomes.

The impact of inflation

When you are planning for many years ahead, it is essential to take account of the effects of inflation. Currently, at the time of writing in 2019, we are in a period of relatively low inflation, 1.8% in the first quarter expected to decrease by the third quarter, largely due to low oil prices (however, watch out for the BREXIT effect, whatever that may be). As prices rise over the years, the money we will have will buy less and less. For example, in the extreme case, if prices double then a fixed amount of money will buy only half as much. The higher the rate of inflation, the more you have to save to reach your income target. The table below will give you an idea of the changes in rates of inflation over the last ten years to 2019.

ear	jan	feb	mar	apr	may	jun	jul	aug	sep	oct	nov	dec	ann
2019	1.8%												
2018	3%	2.7%	2.4%	2.4%	2.4%	2.4%	2.5%	2.6%	2.4%	2.4%	2.3%	2.1%	2.5%
2017	1.8%	2.3%	2.3%	2.7%	2.9%	2.7%	2.6%	2.9%	2.9%	3%	3.1%	2.9%	2.7%
2016	0.3%	0.3%	0.5%	0.3%	0.3%	0.4%	0.6%	0.6%	1%	0.9%	1.2%	1.6%	0.7%
2015	0.3%	0%	0%	-0.2%	0.1%	0%	0.1%	0.1%	-0.1%	-0.1%	0.2%	0.2%	0%
2014	2%	1.7%	1.6%	1.8%	1.5%	1.9%	1.6%	1.5%	1.2%	1.3%	0.9%	0.5%	1.5%
2013	2.6%	2.8%	2.8%	2.4%	2.7%	2.9%	2.8%	2.7%	2.7%	2.2%	2.1%	2%	2.6%
2012	3.6%	3.4%	3.5%	3%	2.7%	2.4%	2.5%	2.5%	2.2%	2.6%	2.7%	2.6%	2.8%
2011	4%	4.3%	3.9%	4.5%	4.5%	4.2%	4.5%	4.5%	5.1%	5%	4.8%	4.3%	4.5%
2010	3.4%	3%	3.4%	3.7%	3.5%	3.2%	3%	3.2%	3.1%	3.2%	3.2%	3.6%	3.3%
2009	3%	3.1%	2.9%	2.4%	2.1%	1.8%	1.9%	1.5%	1.2%	1.5%	2%	2.9%	2

Some pension schemes give you automatic protection against inflation, but many don't and it is largely up to you to decide what protection to build into your planning. The first step is to be aware what effect inflation might have. Fortunately, pension statements and projections these days must all be adjusted for inflation so that figures you are given are expressed in today's money. This gives you an idea of the standard of living you might expect and helps you assess the amount that you need to save. Providers of non-pension investments (such as unit trusts and investment trusts (see later chapters) do not have to give you statements and projections adjusted for inflation. If you use these other investments for your retirement then you will have to make your own adjustments. You can do this using the table below.

Value in today's money of £1,000 you receive in the future

Average rate of inflation

Number of years until you receive the money	2.5% a year	5% a year	7.5% a year	10% a year
5	£884	£784	£697	£621
10	£781	£614	£485	£386
15	£690	£481	£338	£239
20	£610	£377	£235	£149
25	£539	£295	£164	£92
30	£477	£231	£114	£57
35	£421	£181	£80	£36
40	£372	£142	£55	£22
45	£329	£111	£39	£14
50	£291	£87	£39	£9

The above should be a good guide. If you require more detailed forecasting you should go to www.ons.gov.uk (Office of National Statistics).

In the next chapters we will be discussing the various sources of pensions, starting with the all-important State Pension.

****

Chapter 11

Sources of Pensions-A Summary

Sources of pension savings- The State Pension

In brief, the State Pension system is based on National Insurance contributions, payments made by an individual which funds today's pension payments and for those who are young the future contributions will foot their pension bill. Therefore, the state pension system is not a savings scheme it is a pay-as-you-go system.

Pensions are a major area of government spending and are becoming more and more so. Protecting pensions against inflationary increases have put pressure on respective governments, along with the introduction of a second tier-pension, the State second pension (S2P).

The problems of pension provision are set to increase with the numbers of older people outnumbering those in active work, leading to an imbalance in provision. The biggest dilemma facing the government, and future governments, is the problem of convincing people to save for their pensions, therefore taking some of the burden off the state.

As we have seen from the statistics in the chapter 9, those most at risk in terms of retirement poverty are the lower earners, who quite often do not build up enough contributions to gain a state pension, those who contribute to a state pension but cannot save enough to contribute to a private scheme and disabled people who cannot work or carers who also cannot work. The above is not an exclusive list. The government has recognised the difficulties faced by these groups and has, along the way, introduced the state second pension and pension credits.

The over 80 pension

This is a non-contributory pension for people aged 80 or over with little or no state pension. If you are 80 or over, not getting or getting a reduced state pension because you have not paid enough National Insurance contributions (NI) and are currently living in England, Scotland or Wales and have been doing so for a total of 10 years or more in any continuous period of 20 years before or after your 80th birthday, you could claim the over 80 pension. The maximum amount of the over 80 state pension that you can get is currently £75.50 per week (2019/20).

Occupational pensions

Occupational pension schemes are a very important source of income. With Occupational pension schemes the contract is between the company and the pension provider. With Group Personal Pension Schemes although the employer chooses the company the contract is between the employee and the pension company.

Occupational pension Schemes are one of the best ways to pay into a pension scheme as the employer has to contribute a significant amount to the pot. Over the years the amounts paid into occupational pension schemes has increased significantly. Although there have been a number of incidences of occupational schemes being wound up this is relatively small and they remain a key source of retirement income.

From October 2012, it has been compulsory for employers to provide an occupational pension scheme, Auto Enrolment. For the first time, employers are obliged to:

- enrol most of their workforce into a pension scheme; and
- make employer pension contributions

This affects all employers in the UK, regardless of the number of individuals that they employ. Anyone who is classed as a 'worker' for National Minimum Wage purposes is included in the new pension regime.

This has been introduced in stages, and each employer was given a 'staging date' determined by how many employees they had as at April 1st 2012.

Stakeholder schemes
Stakeholder pension schemes are designed for those people who do not have an employer, or had an employer who did not have an occupational scheme. They therefore cannot pay into an occupational scheme. If an employer did not offer an occupational scheme (many small employers were exempt) they had to arrange access to a stakeholder scheme. Employees did not have to join an occupational scheme offered by employers, instead they could join a stakeholder scheme. Likewise, self-employed people can also join a stakeholder scheme.

Stakeholder schemes have a contribution limit-this being currently £3,600 per year. Anyone who is not earning can also pay into a scheme, up to the limit above. You pay money to a pension provider (eg an insurance company, bank or building society) who invests it (eg in shares).These are a type of personal pension but they have to meet some minimum standards set by the government. These include:

- management charges can't be more than 1.5% of the fund's value for the first 10 years and 1% after that
- you must be able to start and stop payments when you want or switch providers without being charged
- they have to meet certain security standards, eg have independent trustees and auditors.

How much can be invested in a stakeholder pension?

There is no limit to the amount that can be invested in a stakeholder pension scheme. However, tax relief can only be obtained on contributions up to a maximum annual contribution limit (known as an individual's 'annual allowance'). For the tax year 2019/20, this is set at the lower of 100% of an individual's UK earnings or £40,000 per annum. Carry forward of unused allowances may be permitted in some circumstances. It is possible to contribute up to £3,600 per year (including tax relief) into a stakeholder pension scheme even if a person is not earning. A member of an occupational pension scheme may also contribute to a stakeholder pension scheme. You can start making payments into a stakeholder pension from £20 per month. You can pay weekly or monthly. If you don't want to make regular payments you can pay lump sums any time you want.

The rules for stakeholder pensions changed on 1 October 2012. If you're starting a new job now or returning to one, your employer doesn't have to offer you access to a stakeholder pension scheme. They now have to offer entry through automatic enrolment. If you're in a stakeholder pension scheme that was arranged by your employer before 1 October 2012, they must continue to take and pay contributions from your wages. This arrangement is in place until:

- you ask them to stop
- you stop paying contributions at regular intervals
- you leave your job

If you leave your job or change to another personal pension, the money they have paid in stays in your pension pot unless you have it transferred to a different pension provider.

Other ways to save for retirement

The government offers certain tax advantages to encourage pension saving. However, the most advantageous savings plan is the Individual Savings Account (ISA), the current limit being £20,000 in 2019/20. In addition, you might have regular savings accounts, your home or a second home. All of these possibilities must be factored in when arriving at an adequate retirement income.

****

Chapter 12

Private Pension Savings-General

The lifetime allowance

There is a single lifetime limit on the amount of savings that a person can build up through various pension schemes and plans that are subject to tax relief. (This excludes the state pension). The lifetime allowance is £1,055,000m from April 2019.

The lifetime allowance applies to savings in all types of pension schemes including occupational pensions and stakeholder schemes. There are, broadly, two types of scheme or plan:

- Defined contribution-with these types of schemes money goes in and is invested with the fund used to buy a pension. Basically, if the fund at retirement is £200,000 then £200,000 lifetime allowance has been used up

- Defined benefit-in this type of scheme, a person is promised a pension of a certain amount usually worked out on the basis of salary before retirement and the length of time that you have been in the scheme. The equation for working out lifetime benefit in this type of scheme is a little more complicated. The pension is first converted into a notional sum (the amount of money it is reckoned is needed to buy a pension of that size). The government sets out a factor that it says will be needed to make the conversion which it has said is 20. If the pension is £20,000 then this is calculated as £20,000 times £20,000 which is £400,000. Therefore £400,000 will be used up from the lifetime allowance.

Protecting the Lifetime Allowance

The standard lifetime allowance is £1,055,000 million on 6 April 2019. But you may be able to protect your pension(s) from these reductions.

There are 3 protections you can apply for.

Protection	What it does	Can I keep building up my pension(s)?
Individual protection 2016	Protects your lifetime allowance to the lower of: - the value of your pension(s) at 5 April 2016- £1.25 million	Yes. But you must pay tax on money taken from your pension(s) that exceed your protected lifetime allowance.
Fixed protection 2016	Fixes your lifetime allowance at £1.25 million.	No, except in limited circumstances. If you do, you'll: - lose your fixed protection 2016 - pay tax on any pension(s) above the standard lifetime allowance when you take your pension
Individual protection 2014	Protects your lifetime allowance to the lower of: - the value of your pension(s) at 5 April 2014 1- £.5 million	Yes. But you must pay tax on money taken from your pension(s) that exceed your protected lifetime allowance.

For more detailed information about Pension protection Schemes go to: www.gov.uk/guidance/pension-schemes-protect-your-lifetime-allowance

The annual allowance

The annual allowance (amount that an individual can contribute to a pension) is £40,000 (April 2019). This is the amount that pension savings may increase each year whether through contributions paid in or to promised benefits. In addition, you can carry forward unused allowances from three years previously the annual allowance will not start in the year a person starts their pension or die. This gives a person scope to make large last-minute additions to their fund. If at retirement the value of a pension exceeds the lifetime allowance there will be an income tax charge of 55% on the excess if it is taken as a lump sum, or 25% if it is left in the scheme to be taken as a pension, which is taxable as income. If the increase in the value of savings in any year exceeds the annual allowance, the excess is taxed at 40%.

Limits to benefits and contributions

The present benefit and contribution limits have been scrapped. The only remaining restrictions are:

- Contributions-the maximum that can be paid in each year is either the amount equal to taxable earnings or £3,600 whichever is the greater
- Tax free lump sum-at retirement a person can take up to one quarter of the value of the total pension fund as a tax free lump sum

Taking a pension

Savings do not have to be converted into pension in one go. This can be staggered and pension income can be increased as a person winds down from work.

For each tranche of pension started before 75, there is a range of choices. This will depend on the rules of each individual scheme. A person can:

- Have a pension paid direct from an occupational pension scheme
- Use a pension fund to purchase an annuity to provide a pension for the rest of life
- Use part of the pension to buy a limited period annuity lasting just five years leaving the rest invested
- Opt for income drawdown which allows taking of a pension whilst leaving the rest invested. The tax-free lump sum could be taken and the rest left invested. The maximum income will be 120% of a standard annuity rate published by the Financial Conduct Authority. On death the remaining pension fund can be used to provide pensions for dependants or paid to survivors as a lump sum, taxed at 35%.

From 6 April 2015, where the member dies before the age of 75, spouses or other beneficiaries who inherit joint life or guaranteed term annuities will no longer be taxed on the income. This aligns their treatment with dependant drawdown pensions.

It was also confirmed that drawdown pensions paid to spouses, or other dependants or nominees, would be tax-free where the member died before reaching the age of 75 and the pension first comes into payment on or after 6 April 2015. The fund can also be passed on tax-free as a lump sum, rather than potentially being subject to a 55% charge.

Not all dependant pensions will benefit from the tax exemption, however. Where the member dies before the age of 75 with either uncrystallised funds or a drawdown fund, if the beneficiary chooses to buy an annuity with the fund rather than go into drawdown, this will remain fully taxable. Similarly, there is no provision for making inherited scheme pensions (eg widow's pensions from final salary schemes) tax-free. Where the member dies after reaching the age of 75, all dependant pensions remain taxable, as they are under the current rules. Dependants who are already in receipt of annuities before 6 April 2015 will remain taxed on them in the same way as dependant drawdown pensions.

When a person reaches 75 years of age, they must opt for one of the following choices:

- Have a pension paid direct from an occupational scheme
- Use the pension fund to buy an annuity to provide a pension for the rest of life or
- Opt for an Alternatively Secured Pension or ASP. This is pension draw down but with the maximum income limited to 90% of the annuity rate for a 75 year old. On death, the remaining fund can be used to provide dependants pensions or, if there are no dependants, left to a charity or absorbed into the scheme to help other people's pensions. The person(s) whose pensions are to be enhanced can be nominated by the person whose pension it is.

We will be discussing options for taking pensions in more depth in Chapter 15

****

Chapter 13

Choosing a Personal Pension Plan

There is a wide choice of personal pension schemes on offer. One common denominator is that the schemes are now heavily regulated by both the government and the Financial Conduct Authority. Most schemes will accept either a monthly contribution or a one-off lump sum payment per annum. The majority of schemes will allow a person to increase contributions. It is important to look for a plan that will allow a person to miss payments, in case of unemployment, sickness etc, without penalty.

Investments

Plans which allow individuals to choose their own investments are called' Self-invested Personal Pensions' (SIIPS) (see below). A person will build up their own fund of personal investments from a wide range of options such as shares, gilts, property and other areas. However, unless an individual has a large sum to invest, this is unlikely to be a wise bet. Pension companies can offer their own expertise and usually have far greater knowledge than the individual.

Self-invested Personal Pensions (SIPPs)

A self-invested personal pension (SIPP) is a pension 'wrapper' that holds investments until you retire and start to draw a retirement income. It is a type of personal pension and works in a similar way to a standard personal pension. The main difference is that with a SIPP, you have more flexibility with the investments you can choose.

How it works

SIPPs aren't for everyone. Get advice if you're thinking about this type of personal pension. With standard personal pension schemes, your investments are managed for you within the pooled fund you have chosen. SIPPs are a form of personal pension that give you the freedom to choose and manage your own investments. Another option is to pay an authorised investment manager to make the decisions for you.

SIPPs are designed for people who want to manage their own fund by dealing with, and switching, their investments when they want to. SIPPs can also have higher charges than other personal pensions or stakeholder pensions. For these reasons, SIPPs tend to be more suitable for large funds and for people who are experienced in investing.

What you can and can't invest in

Most SIPPs allow you to select from a range of assets, such as:

- Unit trusts.
- Investment trusts.
- Government securities.
- Insurance company funds.
- Traded endowment policies.
- Some National Savings and Investment products.
- Deposit accounts with banks and building societies.
- Commercial property (such as offices, shops or factory premises).

- Individual stocks and shares quoted on a recognised UK or overseas stock exchange.

These aren't all of the investment options that are available – different SIPP providers offer different investment options. It's unlikely that you'll be able to invest directly in residential property within a SIPP. Residential property can't be held directly in a SIPP with the tax advantages that usually accompany pension investments. But, subject to some restrictions, including on personal use, residential property can be held in a SIPP through certain types of collective investments, such as real estate investment trusts, without losing the tax advantages.

How you access money in your SIPP
New rules introduced in April 2015 mean you can access and use your pension pot in any way you wish from age 55, (however, see below-accessing your pension funds to finance your business).

There's a lot to weigh up when working out which option or combination will provide you and any dependants with a reliable and tax-efficient income throughout your retirement. Be sure to use the free, government-backed Pension Wise service to help you understand your options or get financial advice.

As mentioned you should note that in 2019, the **Money and Pensions Service** will be replacing Pension Wise, The Money Advice Service and the Pensions Advisory Service, which will all be under the new umbrella. For further information about the timing of this go to their website:
www.moneyandpensionsservice.org.uk

Small Self-Administered Schemes (Ssas)

A SSAS is essentially an employer sponsored pension scheme with fewer than 12 people, where at least one member is connected with another, or with a trustee or the sponsoring employer, and where some or all of the scheme assets are invested other than in insurance policies.

Every registered pension scheme is required to have a Scheme Administrator. If a Scheme Administrator is not appointed, then the Scheme trustees will normally become the Scheme Administrator by default. The Scheme Administrator must enrol online with HMRC before they can register the SSAS. Contributions to the SSAS must not be paid by either the employer or a member until the scheme has been registered with HM Revenue and Customs.

Any contributions, even if they are only paid to the Trustees' bank account, before the scheme is registered will not receive tax relief. The managing trustees must open a Scheme bank account. Contributions from the company (and the members) are paid into the bank account before they are invested at the managing trustees' discretion (subject to certain restrictions).

The structure of a Small Self-Administered Scheme could, for example, be as follows:

- Company and member payments
- Trustees' bank account
- Insurance Company investments

Self-administered part

– Commercial property eg. company premises.

– Loans to employer.

–Deposit accounts.

– Open Ended Investment Companies (OEICs).

– Stock Exchange

– e.g. equities.

– Securities, etc

– e.g. gilts.

– Trustee Investment Bond.

There are clear benefits to holding assets under a registered pension scheme. For example, no capital gains tax liability arises when scheme assets are sold. On the other hand, when personally-held assets are sold this can trigger a Capital Gains Tax liability. A SSAS:

- Gives the managing trustees wide investment powers.
- Is a possible source of loan capital to the company for business expansion purposes, which may help minimise reliance on a third party (eg. bank).
- May be able to buy the company's premises – the SSAS managing trustees act as the landlord, meaning that the members retain control.
- Can be a possible source of equity capital for business expansion purposes which could avoid partial surrender of control to external interests.
- Is a vehicle for the managing trustees to back their investment judgement. A SSAS generally appeals to controlling directors who want
- To retain control over their pension benefits.
- To use the self-investment facility to help the company's development.
- A greater say in the way pension payments are invested

Releasing funds to finance business

One of the important points here is that, if the scheme is a small self-administered scheme it can be accessed to provide funds for a business, even if you are under the age of 55. This is known as 'pension-led funding'. Both SIIP's and SSAS's serve as an appropriate vehicle for this.

To effect pension-led funding you set up a sale and leaseback type arrangement whereby your pension buys assets from your business or loans money to your business secured against your retirement funds. However, it should be noted that there are advantages and disadvantages of doing this so you would need to talk the matter through with a pension provider with knowledge of this area. Scottish Widows is one such provider. There are many more. A reputable financial advisor will be able to point you in the right direction.

Fees and other charges

Those who invest your money on your behalf don't work for nothing. Fees are charged. The rate of interest offered will reflect the ultimate charge and there will probably be an administration fee too. Some plans have very complicated charging structures and it is very important that these are understood before decisions are made.

Other benefits from a personal pension

A personal pension scheme does not automatically offer a package of benefits in addition to the actual pension. Any additional benefits have to be paid for. The range of extra benefits includes lump sum life cover for dependants if death occurs before retirement, a pension for widow or widower or other partner, a waiver of contributions if there is an inability to work and a pension paid early if sickness or disability prevents working until retirement age.

A contracted out personal pension must allow for a widow's or widower's pension to be payable if the widow or widower is over 45 years of age, or is younger than 45 but qualifies for child benefit. The pension would be whatever amount can be bought by the fund built up through investing the contracting-out rebates. The widow or widower has an open market option, which gives him or her a right to shop around for a different pension provider rather than remain with the existing provider.

The pension could cease if the widow or widower remarries while under the state pension age, or ceases to be eligible for child benefit whilst still under 45. This depends on the terms of the contract at the time of death.

A contracted out widow's or widower's pension built up before 6th April 1997 must be increased each year in line with inflation, up to a maximum of 3% a year. For post April 1997 pensions this must be up to 5% per year and after 6th April 2005, pensions taken out don't have to increase at all.

With the exception of contracted out plans, a person must choose at the time of taking out the plan which death benefits to have as part of the scheme. Broadly, they should be in line with the benefits mentioned above.

Retirement due to ill-health
If a person has to retire due to ill-health, a pension can be taken from a personal plan at any age. However, a person's inability to work must be clearly demonstrated and backed up with a professional opinion.

Taking a pension early will result in a reduced pension because what is in the pot will be less. However, there are ways of mitigating this, one way to ensure that a waiver of premiums in the event of sickness is included in the pension. In this way the plan will continue to grow even though a person is ill. Another way is to take out permanent disability insurance. This insurance will guarantee that the pension that you will get when you cannot work will at least be a minimum amount.

The Pension Protection Fund

Members of defined benefit occupational pension schemes are protected through the PPF, which will pay regular compensation, based on your pension amount, if the company becomes insolvent and the pension scheme doesn't have enough money to pay your pension. The PPF applies to most defined benefit schemes where the employer became insolvent after 6th April 2005. You should check with the PPF about levels of compensation.

The Financial Assistance Scheme

If you are an individual scheme member and have lost out on your pension as a result of your scheme winding up after 1st January 1997 and the introduction of PPF, you may be able to get financial help from the FAS, which is administered by the Pension Protection Fund, if:

- your defined benefit scheme was under funded and
- your employer is insolvent, no longer exists or has entered into a valid compromise agreement with the trustees of the pension fund to avoid insolvency; or
- in some circumstances, your final salary scheme was wound up because it could not pay members benefits even if the employer continues trading.

In the case of fraud or theft

If the shortfall in your company pension scheme was due to Fraud or theft, it may be possible to recover some of the money through the PPF who operate what is known as the Fraud Compensation Scheme.

The Pension Tracing Service

If you think that you may have an old pension but are not sure of the details, the Pension Tracing Service, part of the Pension Service, may be able to help. They can be contacted on 0800 1223 170 (general enquiries) and will give you full details of their scheme and also will tell you what they need from you in order to trace the pension. www.pensiontracingservice.com.

****

Chapter 14

Pensions and Benefits for Dependants

State pensions

If you die before your spouse or civil partner has reached state pension age there may be some entitlement to state bereavement benefits if you have built up the appropriate NI contributions in the years prior to your death. The following may be available:

- Bereavement payment. This is a tax-free lump sum of £2500 (Standard rate for deaths occurring after 6th April 2017) or £3,500 higher rate.

- Widowed Parent's Allowance. This is a taxable income (£119.90 a week (2019/20) plus half of any additional state pension (S2P) you had built up. The payment continues until the youngest child ceases to be dependant or until your widow, widower or civil partner, enters a new marriage or civil partnership or starts to live with someone as if they were married or registered. Your spouse or civil partner might also be able to claim Child Tax Credit (CTC, a means tested state benefit available to households with children).

- Bereavement allowance. This is a regular taxable payment payable to spouses and civil partners over age 45 without any dependant children. The amount increases with their age. This is payable for a maximum of 52 weeks and will cease if a spouse or civil partner remarries.

Death after retirement

If you die after you and your spouse/civil partner have both reached State Pension age help is given through the State pension system. Your spouse or partner, if they do not receive a full basic pension in their own right, may be able to make up the pension to the full single person's rate, currently £129.20 per week (2019/20) by using your contribution record. In addition, they can inherit half of any additional State Pension you had built up.

To find out more about bereavement benefits contact your local jobcentre plus, if you are of working age at www.direct.gov.uk. Advice on a full range of bereavement benefits for those who are retired can also be obtained here.

Occupational and personal schemes

Occupational and personal schemes may also offer pensions and lump sum pay-outs for your survivors when you die. Schemes can pay pensions to your dependants (but not anyone who was not dependant or co-dependant on you) whether you die before or after you started your pension. This means your husband, wife, civil partner, children under the age of 23 or, if older, dependant on you because of physical or mental impairment.

Also, anyone else financially dependant on you can benefit. Under the tax rules, all the dependants pensions added together must not come to more than the retirement pension you would have been entitled to, but otherwise there is no limit on the amount of any one pension, although individual scheme rules may set some limits.

117

Dependant's pensions from occupational salary-related schemes

Subject to tax rules governing such schemes, a scheme can set its own rules about how much pension it will provide for dependants. Typically, a scheme will provide a pension for a widow, widower, civil partner or unmarried partner on:

- death before you have started your pension
- death after you have started your pension.
- This will typically be half or two thirds of the pension that you were entitled to at the time of your death. The pension must be increased in line with inflation. If you have been contracted out through a salary related pension scheme before April 1977, the scheme must pay a guaranteed minimum pension (GMP) to the person entitled equal to half the GMP's you had built up.

Lump sum death benefits

The options available to your beneficiaries after you die will depend on how you choose to take your pension and at what age you die. In the event of your death whilst in drawdown your beneficiaries will have the following options under the current rules:

- **Take the pension as a lump sum** Any beneficiary can inherit some or all of your remaining fund. They can do what they like with it. This payment will be tax free if you die before reaching age 75, or taxed at the beneficiary's marginal rate of income tax if after.
- **Continue with drawdown** A dependant or nominated beneficiary can continue to receive your fund as drawdown. Income from which will be tax free if you die

before reaching age 75, or taxed at the beneficiary's marginal rate of income tax if after.

- **Convert the drawdown fund to a lifetime annuity** A dependant or nominated beneficiary can use your remaining drawdown fund to purchase a lifetime annuity. The income will be tax free if you die before reaching age 75, or taxed at the beneficiary's marginal rate of income tax if after.

Pensions are typically held in trust outside your estate and so in most cases are free of inheritance tax (IHT). Death benefits set up more than two years after death may lose their tax-free status. If you make a pension contribution or reduce the income you are drawing from your drawdown plan while in ill health or within two years of death the funds may still be liable to IHT. Tax charges may also apply if you exceed the lifetime allowance and die before age 75.

This information is based on 6 April 2019 pension rules and is subject to change. Tax rules & benefits can change and their value will depend on your personal circumstances.

****

Chapter 15

Pensions-Options for Retirement and Tax Implications for Private Pensions

---

Retirement options and taxation of pensions

As you will know by now, changes introduced from April 2015 give you freedom over how you can access your pension savings if you're 55 or over and have a pension based on how much has been paid into your pot (such as a defined contribution, money purchase or cash balance scheme).

Options for using your pension pot

Depending on your age and personal circumstances some or all of the options outlined below could be suitable for you. Your main options are:

1. Keep your pension savings where they are and take them later on in life.
2. Use your pension pot to get a guaranteed income for life – called a Lifetime annuity. The income is taxable, but you can choose to take up to 25% of your pot as a one-off tax-free lump sum at the outset.
3. Use your pension pot to provide a Flexible retirement income, take 25% of your pension pot (or 25% of the amount you allocate for this option) as a tax-free lump sum, then use the rest to provide a regular taxable income.

4. Take a number of lump sums – the first 25% of each cash withdrawal from your pot will be tax-free. The rest will be taxed.
5. Take your pension pot in one go – the first 25% will be tax-free and the rest is taxable.
6. Mix your options – choose any combination of the above, using different parts of your pot or separate pots.

We will now look at each of these six options, and the implications, in turn.

1. Keep your pension savings where they are

With this option, your pot continues to grow tax-free until you need it – potentially providing more income once you start taking money out. You (and your employer) can continue making contributions however there are restrictions on how much you can save each year and over a lifetime and still receive tax relief.

In most cases you can get tax relief on pension contributions, including any employer contributions, on the lower of 100% of your earnings or up to £40,000 each year (2019-20 tax year) until age 75. However, if you are a high earner the limit on how much tax-free money you can build up in your pension in any one year depends on your 'adjusted income'. If you don't pay Income Tax, you can still get tax relief on up to £3,600 of pension savings each year until age 75.

However, you will need to check with your pension scheme or provider whether there are any restrictions or charges for changing your retirement date, and the process and deadline for telling them. You need to know whether there are any costs for leaving your pot where it is – some providers charge an administration fee for continuing to manage your pension. Check that you won't lose any valuable income guarantees – for example, a guaranteed annuity rate – if you delay your retirement date.

One other important point is that the money you have saved into your pension pot could continue to grow, but it could also go down in value, as with any investment. Remember to review where your pot is invested as you get closer to the time you want to retire and arrange to move it to less risky funds if necessary.

If you want your pot to remain invested after the age of 75, you'll need to check that your pension scheme or provider will allow this. If not, you may need to transfer to another scheme or provider who will. Not all pension schemes and providers will allow you to delay. If you want to delay but don't have this option, shop around before moving your pension.

On death, any unused pension pots normally fall outside your estate for Inheritance Tax purposes and can be passed on to any nominated beneficiary. In both cases the money continues to grow tax-free while still invested.

If you die before age 75: Provided the beneficiary takes the money within two years of the provider being notified of the pension holder's death, they can take it as a tax-free lump sum or as tax-free income. If they take it later (whether as a lump sum or income) it will be added to their other income and taxed at the appropriate Income Tax rate.

If you die age 75 or over: When the money is taken out (lump sum or income) it will be added to the beneficiary's income and taxed at the appropriate Income Tax rate. However, if the beneficiary is not an individual but is, for example, a company or trust, any lump sum will be taxed at 45%.

2. Use your pension pot to get a guaranteed income for life

A guaranteed income for life – known as a lifetime annuity – provides you with a guarantee that the money will last as long as you live. Guaranteed lifetime income products include: basic lifetime annuities; Investment-linked annuities.

The options

You can choose to take up to 25% (a quarter) of your pot as a one-off tax-free lump sum at the outset. You use the rest to buy a guaranteed lifetime income – a lifetime annuity – from your provider or another insurance company. You must buy within six months of taking your tax-free lump sum. As a rule of thumb, the older you are when you take out a guaranteed lifetime income product, the higher the income you'll get. You can choose to receive your income monthly, quarterly, half-yearly or yearly, depending on the scheme or provider. This type of income is taxable.

Basic lifetime annuities

Basic lifetime annuities offer a range of income options designed to match different personal circumstances. You need to decide whether you want:

- one that provides a guaranteed income for you only and stops when you die –a single life annuity, or one that also provides an income for life for a dependant or other nominated beneficiary after you die – a joint life annuity (normally provides a lower regular income as it's designed to pay out for longer)
- payments to continue to a nominated beneficiary for a set number of years (for example 10 years) from the time the guaranteed income starts, in case you die

123

unexpectedly early – called a guarantee period (can be combined with a single or joint life annuity). For example, if you opt for a guarantee period of 10 years and die after two years, the payments to a nominated beneficiary would continue for eight years.

- payments fixed at the same amount throughout your life – a level annuity, or payments to be lower than a level annuity to start with but rise over time by set amounts – an escalating annuity – or in line with inflation – an inflation-linked annuity.

- value protection – less commonly used and likely to reduce the amount of income you receive, but designed to pay your nominated beneficiary the value of the pot used to buy the guaranteed lifetime income less income already paid out when you die.

Investment-linked annuities

If you're willing to take more risk in return for a potentially higher income, you could opt for an income that is investment-linked (known as an investment-linked annuity). The income you receive rises and falls in line with the value of investments that you choose when you purchase your product. So while it could pay more over the longer term than a basic annuity, your income could also fall.

Many investment-linked annuities guarantee a minimum income if the fund's performance is weak. With investment-linked annuities you can also have a dependant's pension, guarantee periods, value protection and higher rates if you have a short life expectancy due to poor health or lifestyle. Some investment-linked annuities allow you to change your investment options or allow you to take lower payments later.

Although you can't change your guaranteed income back into a pension pot, the government has announced changes which to come into force in early 2017, that may allow you to sell your product for a cash lump sum on which you may have to pay Income Tax. How much tax you pay would depend on the value of your product, and your overall income in that year.

Think carefully about whether you need to provide an income for your partner or another dependant on your death. Consider whether you should take a product which provides an increasing income. Inflation (the general rise in price of goods and services over time) can significantly reduce your standard of living over time. Investment-linked annuities offer the chance of a higher income – but only by taking extra risk. Your income could reduce if the fund doesn't perform as expected. If you're considering this option look at what your provider can offer then get financial advice.

If you buy guaranteed income with money from a pension pot you've already used for another income option (e.g. to provide a flexible retirement income) you can't take a further tax-free lump sum – even if you chose not to take a tax-free lump sum with the other option.

Not all pension schemes and providers offer guaranteed lifetime income products. Some may only offer one type, or offer to buy one on your behalf. Whatever the case, shop around before deciding who to go with – you're likely to get a better income than sticking with your current provider.

Tax

You will have to pay tax on the income you receive, in the same way you pay tax on your salary. How much you pay depends on your total income and the Income Tax rate that applies to you. Your provider will take tax off your income before you receive it

Because they won't know your overall income they will use an emergency tax code to start with. This means you may pay too much tax initially and have to claim the money back – or you may owe more tax if you have other sources of income. If the value of all of your pension savings is above £1,055,000m (2019-20 tax year) and these savings haven't already been assessed against the Lifetime allowance, further tax charges may apply when you access your pension pot.

Tax relief on future pension savings

After buying a guaranteed income product you can in most cases continue to get tax relief on pension savings of up to the Annual allowance of £40,000 (2019-20). However, if you buy a lifetime annuity which could decrease such as an investment-linked annuity, the maximum future defined contribution pension savings that can be made in a year that qualifies for tax relief is limited to the lower of £10,000 (the Money purchase annual allowance) or 100% of your earnings. If you want to carry on saving into a pension this option may not be suitable.

On death, if you have a single life guaranteed income product and no other features, your pension stops when you die. Otherwise, the tax rules vary depending on your age as shown below.

If you die before age 75: Income from a joint guaranteed income product will be paid to your dependant or other nominated beneficiary tax-free for the rest of their life. If you die within a guarantee period the remaining payments will pass tax-free to your nominated beneficiary then stop when the guarantee period ends. Any lump sum payment due from a value protected guaranteed lifetime income product will be paid tax-free. It will also normally fall outside your estate for Inheritance Tax purposes.

If you die age 75 or over: Income from a joint guaranteed income product or a continuing guarantee period will be added to the beneficiary's overall income and taxed at the appropriate Income Tax rate. Joint payments will stop when your dependant or other beneficiary dies and any guarantee period payments stop when the guarantee period ends. Any lump sum due from a value protected guaranteed income product will be added to the beneficiary's overall income and taxed at the appropriate Income Tax rate. Lump sums due from a value protected guaranteed income product normally fall outside your estate for Inheritance Tax purpose.

3. Use your pension pot to provide a flexible retirement income

You can move all or some of your pension pot into an investment specifically designed to provide an income for your retirement . The income isn't guaranteed but you have flexibility to make changes. This is sometimes called 'Flexi-access drawdown'.

You can choose to take up to 25% (a quarter) of your pension pot as a tax-free lump sum. You then move the rest within six months into one or more funds (or other assets) that allow you to take income at times to suit you – e.g. monthly, quarterly, yearly or irregular withdrawals. Most people use it to take a regular income. If you don't move the rest of your money within the six months, you'll be charged tax (normally 55% of the un-transferred fund value). Once you've taken your tax-free lump sum, you can start taking the income right away, or wait until a later date. The income is taxable.

Unlike with a guaranteed income for life (a lifetime annuity), the retirement income you receive from a flexible retirement income product is not guaranteed to last as long as you live, so you should think carefully about how much you withdraw.

Deciding how much income you can afford to take needs careful planning – it depends on how much money you put in from your pension pot, the performance of the funds, what other sources of income you have, and whether you want to provide for a dependant or someone else after you die. It also depends on how long you will live. Your retirement income could fall or even run out if you take too much too soon and start eating into the money you originally invested to produce the income – especially if stock markets fall. Investment choice is key – you will need to review where your money is invested regularly to ensure it continues to meet your long-term retirement income needs. Investments can fall as well as rise – you'll need to know how you'll cope if your income suddenly drops.

Not all pension schemes and providers offer flexible retirement income products. If yours doesn't, you can transfer your pension pot to another provider who does but again there may be a fee to do so. Different providers will offer different features and charging structures on their products – and the choice is likely to increase.

You pay tax on the income withdrawals (outside the tax-free cash allowance). How much tax you pay depends on your total income and the Income Tax rate that applies to you. Your provider will take tax off your income payments in advance. Because they won't know your overall income they will use an emergency tax code to start with which means you may initially pay too much tax – and have to claim the money back – or you may owe more tax if you have other sources of income. If you have other income, you'll need to plan carefully how much flexible retirement income to take, to avoid pushing yourself into a higher tax bracket.

Tax relief on future pension savings

Once you have taken any money from your flexible retirement income product, the maximum future defined contribution pension savings that can be made in a year that qualifies for tax relief is limited to the lower of £4,000 (the Money purchase annual allowance – down from the usual £40,000 Annual allowance in 2019-20) or 100% of your earnings. If you want to carry on building up your pension pot, this may influence when you start taking your flexible retirement income. The tax relief you get for future pension savings is not affected if you take the tax-free lump sum but no income. On death, any remaining flexible retirement income funds when you die normally fall outside your estate for Inheritance Tax purposes.

If you die before age 75: Anything remaining in your fund passed to a nominated beneficiary within two years of notifying the provider of the pension holder's death will be tax-free whether they take it as a lump sum or as income. If it is over two years any money paid will be added to the beneficiary's income and taxed at their appropriate rate.

If you die age 75 or above: Anything remaining in your fund that you pass on – either as a lump sum or income – will be taxed at the beneficiary's appropriate Income Tax rate.

4. Take your pension pot as a number of lump sums

You can leave your money in your pension pot and take lump sums from it when you need it, until your money runs out or you choose another option.

You take cash from your pension pot as and when you need it and leave the rest invested where it can continue to grow tax-free. For each cash withdrawal the first 25% (quarter) will be tax-free and the rest is taxable. There may be charges each time you make a cash withdrawal and/or limits on how many withdrawals you can make each year. Unlike with the flexible retirement income option your pot isn't re-invested into new funds specifically chosen to pay you a regular income.

This option won't provide a regular income for you, or for any dependant after you die. Your pension pot reduces with each cash withdrawal. The earlier you start taking money out the greater the risk that your money could run out – or what's left won't grow sufficiently to generate the income you need to last you into old age.

Remember, as we saw in chapter 2, the buying power of cash reduces because of rising prices over time (inflation) – using cash sums to fund your long-term retirement isn't advisable. If you plan to use cash withdrawals to make a one-off purchase or to pay down debts, you must also be sure that you have enough left to live on for the rest of your life.

In addition, it is worth noting that this option won't provide a regular retirement income for you or for any dependants after you die.

Not all pension providers or schemes offer the ability to withdraw your pension pot as a number of lump sums. Shop around if you want this option but can't get it with your current provider, as charges and restrictions will vary. You may not be able to use this option if you have primary protection or enhanced protection, and protected rights to a tax-free lump sum of more than £375,000 (protections that relate to the LIfetime Allowance).

Tax

Three-quarters (75%) of each cash withdrawal counts as taxable income. This could increase your tax rate when added to your other income. How much tax you pay depends on your total income and the Income Tax rate that applies to you. Your pension scheme or provider will pay the cash and take off tax in advance. Because they won't know your overall income they will use an emergency tax code to start with. This means you may pay too much tax and have to claim the money back – or you may owe more tax if you have other sources of income. If the value of all of your pension savings is above £1,055,000m and these savings haven't already been assessed against the Lifetime allowance (2019-20 tax year), further tax charges may apply when you access your pension pot. Once you reach age 75, if you have less remaining Lifetime allowance available than the amount you want to withdraw, the amount you will get tax-free will be limited to 25% (a quarter) of your remaining Lifetime allowance, rather than 25% of the amount you are taking out.

Tax relief on future pension savings

Once you have taken a lump sum, the maximum future defined contribution pension savings that can be made in a year that qualifies for tax relief is limited to the lower of £4,000 (the Money purchase annual allowance – down from the £40,000 Annual allowance for most people in 2019-20) or 100% of your earnings. If you want to carry on saving into a pension, this option may not be suitable.

On death any untouched part of your pension pot normally falls outside your estate for Inheritance Tax purposes.

If you die before age 75: Any untouched part of your pension pot will pass tax-free to your nominated beneficiary provided the money is claimed within 2 years of notifying the provider of the pension holder's death. If it is over 2 years the money will be added to the beneficiary's other income and taxed at the appropriate rate.

If you die age 75 or over: Any untouched part of your pension pot that you pass on - either as a lump sum or income - will be added to the beneficiary's overall income and taxed at the appropriate Income Tax rate.

5. Take your pension pot in one go

You no longer have to convert your pension pot into an income if you don't want to. You can take out all of your pension savings in one go if you wish. Cashing in your pension pot will not give you a secure retirement income. Basically, you close your pension pot and withdraw it all as cash. The first 25% (quarter) will be tax-free and the rest will be taxable.

This option won't provide a regular income for you – or for your spouse, civil partner or other dependant after you die. Three-quarters (75%) of the amount you withdraw is taxable income, so there's a strong chance your tax rate would go up when the money is added to your other income. If you choose this option you can't change your mind – so you need to be certain that it's right for you. For many or most people it will be more tax efficient to consider one or more of the other options. If you plan to use the cash to clear debts, buy a holiday, or indulge in a big-ticket item you need to think carefully before committing to this option.

Doing so will reduce the money you will have to live on in retirement, and you could end up with a large tax bill.

In addition, you may not be able to use this option if you have primary protection or enhanced protection, and protected rights to a tax-free lump sum of more than £375,000 (protections that relate to the LIfetime Allowance). It is best to talk to your scheme if you have one or more of these kinds of protection and find out what your options are. There may be charges for cashing in your whole pot. Check with your scheme or provider. Not all pension schemes and providers offer cash withdrawal – shop around then get financial advice if you still want this option after considering its risks, as charges may vary.

Tax relief on future pension savings

Once you have cashed in your pension pot, the maximum future defined contribution pension savings that can be made in a year that qualifies for tax relief is limited to the lower of £4,000 (the Money purchase annual allowance – down from the usual £40,000 Annual allowance which will apply for most people in 2019-20) or 100% of your earnings.

On death, whatever age you die, any money remaining or investments bought with cash taken out of your pension pot will count as part of your estate for Inheritance Tax. By contrast, any part of your pot that was untouched would not normally be liable.

6. Mixing your options

You don't have to choose one option – you can mix and match as you like over time or over your total pension pot, whichever suits your needs. You can also keep saving into a pension if you wish, and get tax relief up to age 75. Which option or combination is right for you will depend on:

- when you stop or reduce your work
- your income objectives and attitude to risk

- your age and health
- the size of your pension pot and other savings
- any pension or other savings of your spouse or partner, if relevant
- the possible effect on your entitlement to State benefits
- whether you have financial dependants
- whether your circumstances are likely to change in the future.

Tax-free lump sums when mixing options

Note that depending on how you access money from your pension pot you may only get one chance to take your tax-free amount. This can be anything up to 25% (a quarter) of the amount you access and must be taken at that time. For example, if you use your whole pension pot to provide a flexible retirement income, you use up your rights to take a tax-free sum at the time you transfer the funds. So whether you choose to take 25% tax-free, or less – or no tax-free sum at all – you can't take a tax-free lump sum later if, for example, you decide to use part of your flexible retirement income fund to buy a guaranteed income for life (an annuity). However, if you only used part of your pot to buy a flexible retirement income and later wanted to use some or all of the remaining part of your pension pot to buy a regular income for life (a lifetime annuity), you could take up to 25% of that money as tax-free cash.

On death, the same rules apply for passing on your remaining pension as already set out for each option.

For more advice on pensions and tax go to www.pensionsadvisoryservice.org.uk

****

Chapter 16

Reaching Retirement Age

We have discussed many of the issues in this section in previous chapters. Nevertheless it is worth reiterating them as when you reach retirement age you will want to know the practical issues such as how do you claim your pension.

On reaching retirement age, it will be necessary to ensure that all paperwork relating to pension contributions is in order. There are a number of rules that should be observed in order to ensure that any pension due is paid:

- keep all documents relating to pension rights
- start organising any pension due before retirement, this will ensure that any problems are overcome well before retirement

It is very important that communication is kept with all pension providers, and that they have accurate up-to-date records of a person's whereabouts. Each time addresses are changed this should be communicated to all pension providers. If it is impossible to track down an old employer from whom a pension is due, the Pension Schemes Registry can help. The Pensions Regulator is responsible for the Pension Schemes Registry. This was set up in 1990, by the government to help people trace so-called 'lost pensions'. If help is needed this can be obtained by filling in a form which can be accessed on the website of the pensions regulator www.pensionsregulator.gov.uk

How to claim state pension

A letter will be sent to all retiree's about four months before retirement date. This will come from the pension service and will detail how much pension is due. The pension is not paid automatically, it has to be claimed. This can be done by phoning the Pensions Claim Line number included with the letter, or by filling in a claim form BR1. If the person is a married man and the wife is claiming based on the husbands contributions, then form BF225 should be filled in. If the pension is to be deferred it is advisable to contact the Pensions Service in writing as soon as possible at www. pensionsadvisoryservice.org.uk. A late pension claim can be backdated up to twelve months. If a man is claiming for a pension for his wife based on his contributions this can only be backdated six-months.

How the pension is paid

Pensions are paid by the DWP pension direct to a bank account or Post Office Card Account. To find out more about the payment of pensions contact the DWP www.gov.uk/government/organisations/department-for-work-pensions.

Leaving the country

If a person goes abroad for less than six months, they can carry on receiving pension in the normal way. If the trip is for longer then the Pension Service should be contacted and one of the following arrangements can be made to pay a pension: Have it paid into a personal bank account while away; arrange for it to be paid into a Post Office Card Account; arrange for the money to be paid abroad; If a person is living outside of the UK at the time of the annual pension increase they won't qualify for the increase unless they reside in a member country of the European Union or a country with which the UK has an agreement for increasing pensions. It is very important that you check what will happen to your state pension when you move abroad. The DWP International Pension Centre can help on 0191 218 7777, or access advice through their main website www.gov.uk/international-pension-centre.

Pensions from an occupational scheme

Although different schemes have different arrangements, there are similar rules for each scheme. About three months before a person reaches normal retirement age, they should contact the scheme. Either telephone or write enclosing all the details that they will need. The following questions should be asked:

- What pension is due?
- What is the lump-sum entitlement?
- How will the pension be reduced if a lump sum is taken?
- How will the pension be paid, will there be any choices as to frequency?
- Is there a widow's or widowers pension, and if so how will it affect the retirement pension?
- Are there any pensions for other dependants in the event of death?

If a person has been making Additional Voluntary Contributions, then a detailed breakdown of these will be needed.

A pension from a personal plan

In the same way as a pension from an occupational scheme, it is necessary to get in touch with the pension provider about 3-4 months before retirement date.

The main questions that should be asked are:

- How much is the pension fund worth?
- How much pension will the plan provider offer?
- Can an increase be arranged each year and if so how much is the increase?
- What is the maximum lump sum?
- Is there a widow's or widowers or other dependants pension?
- What are the other options if any?
- Can the purchase of an annuity be deferred without affecting the drawing of an income?

Pensions can only be paid by an insurance company or a friendly society so if the pension has been with any other form of provider then it has to be switched before it can be paid.

If there are protected-rights from a contracted out pension plan, these can be, may have to be, treated quite separately from the rest of a pension. Protected rights from a personal pension cannot be paid until a person has reached 60 years of age. A person must, by law, have an open market option enabling protected rights pension to be paid by another provider, if it is desired.

New regulations for pension providers

As we have discussed, at the end of February 2015, the government introduced new regulations that pension providers must abide by. Pension providers will have to give specific risk warnings to savers looking to take advantage of the 2015 reforms. Any regulated company that sells policies that offer a retirement income will have to tell customers about the tax implications of cashing in or investing their pension once the reforms are fully enacted from April 6th 2015. Pension companies must also highlight how a savers health could affect their retirement income. The providers must also provide advice on the effect on benefits and also warn of scams.

Advice schemes for pensions

To help people with the transition, the government introduced a new advice service called Pension Wise. This is administered through The Pensions Advisory Services (TPAS) and the Citizens Advice Bureau. This was rolled out in March and April 2015 (as stated currently being merged into the Money and Pensions Service). Pensioners with defined contribution pension savings-either a workplace money purchase plan or a personal pension plan-will be able to access the scheme. They should be 55 or over or near retirement and can register through the Pension Wise website www.pensionwise.gov.uk.

Customers will have to book an appointment to receive either phone based advice or one to one advice and the sessions will last up to 45 minutes. Guidance will include life expectancy, long term care needs, various pension products from annuities to drawdown and a tax calculator. The guidance is not the same as regulated financial advice, such as how to invest your money but is general guidance.

Beware of Scams

As we all know, there are scammers in every walk of life. This is how they make their living, usually having failed in legitimate enterprise. There have been warnings of increased scamming activity since the chancellor first announced the changes. Basically, scammers cold call people, promising to unlock pensions, luring people with promises of sky high returns on a number of ludicrous schemes, such as investment in property etc. In reality they are running off with your cash, leaving you with a sky high tax bill and no money.

The fundamental rule is: **avoid any cold callers** and those who promise anything at all. Avoid looking for free advice on the internet. **It is all bogus**. Manage your money yourself, after taking advice and guidance from the government scheme or through a financial advisor who is regulated by the Financial Conduct Authority. Always make sure that you are aware of the level of fees charged by financial advisors, as sometimes they can be quite high. Don't feel that you have to rush in if you are over 55. Take your time and consider the options carefully.

The Pensions Dashboard

At the time of writing (2019) the government has announced that it is going ahead with the proposed pensions dashboard. This will be an extremely useful site which will enable workers and retirees to see all of their pensions details, both private and state pensions, on one website. For more information concerning the pensions dashboard and its progress go to pensionsdashboardproject.uk/saver/about-the-pensions-dashboard

Inheriting pensions on death

One important factor is the question of to whom do you leave your pension on death? Are your retirement policies updated in relation to who gets your pensions or is there a danger of the pension being passed on to the wrong person, such as an ex-husband or boyfriend or someone else who you would not like to see receive the pension?

The rise in the number of divorces, remarriages and couples co-habiting, plus a general apathy towards dealing with pensions when retirement is decades away, means many people could inadvertently be handing valuable benefits to former partners.

Pension schemes typically have a form that allows members to name the person they want their benefits to go to when they die "expressions of wishes".

Make sure that all of your details are updated to ensure that any benefits go to the person you want them to go to!

****

USEFUL ORGANISATIONS

MANAGING MONEY

Association of Investment Companies (AITC)
9th Floor
24 Chiswell Street
London
EC1Y 4YY
www.theaic.co.uk
020 7282 555

Debt Management Office
Eastcheap Court
11 Philpot Lane
London EC3M 8UD
www.dmo.gov.uk

Department for Work and Pensions (DWP)
If you ring The Pension Service on 0800 731 7898,
You will be connected to the pension centre covering your area,
Or you can look on the website (www. Thepensionservice.gov.uk

Disability Action Alliance
www.disabilityactionalliance.org.uk
Provides advice and publications on social security benefits
For disabled people.

Financial Ombudsman
Service (FOS)

The Financial Ombudsman Service

Exchange Tower

London E14 9SR

Consumer helpline: 0800 023 4567

www.financialombudsman.org,uk

Financial Conduct Authority (FSA)

12 Endeavour Square,

London,

E20 1JN.

Switchboard: 020 7066 1000

www.fca.gov.uk

HM Revenue & Customs (HMRC)

The government department that deals

With almost all the taxes due in the UK.

Most HMRC leaflets can be obtained

From local tax offices or Tax Enquiry Centres

(look for in the phone book under `Revenue'

or `Government Department')

or Jobcentre Plus offices.

Almost all are also available on the website at:

 https://www.gov.uk/government/collections/hm-revenue-and-

customs-leaflets-factsheets-and-booklets

International Pension Centre

The Pension Service

Tyneview Park

Newcastle upon Tyne NE98 1BA

Tel: 0191 218 7777

Moneyfacts

www.moneyfacts.co.uk

Office of the Public Guardian

The Office of the Public Guardian (OPG) protects people in England and Wales who may not have the mental capacity to make certain decisions for themselves, such as about their health and finance.

www.gov.uk/government/organisations/office-of-the-public-guardian

Pension Tracing Service

www.thepensionservice.gov.uk

Pension Advisory Service

(TPAS)

Helpline: 0800 011 3797

www.pensionsadvisoryservice.org.uk

Tax Help for Older People

Pineapple Business Park

Salway Ash

Bridport

Dorset DT6 5DB

Tel: 01308 488066 www.taxvol.org.uk

KEEPING ACTIVE

Association of British Travel Agents (ABTA)

30 Park Street

London SE1 9EQ

www.abtanet.com

British Franchise Association

(BFA)

British Franchise Association,

85f Park Drive, Milton Park,

Abingdon,

OX14 4RY

01235 820 470

www.thebfa.org

Community volunteering

Do-It-Trust (GB)

www.do-it.org

Cycling UK

Parklands

Railton Road

Guildford

Surrey GU2 9JX

www.cyclinguk.org

Department for Transport

Mobility inclusion

https://www.gov.uk/government/organisations/department-for-transport

Disabled Persons Railcard Office

http://www.disabledpersons-railcard.co.uk

European Health Insurance Card (EHIC)

http://www.nhs.uk/NHSEngland/Healthcareabroad

Learndirect

For free advice about all

Areas of learning and

Training.

Tel: 0800 101 901

www.learndirect.com

Mobility-Motability Car Scheme

Tel: 0300 456 4566

www.motability.co.uk

**National Association of Councils for Voluntary
And Community Action**

The Workstation,

Paternoster Row,

Sheffield

S1 2BX

0114 278 6636

www.navca.org.uk

National Federation of Women's Institutes

104 New Kings Road

London SW6 4LY

Tel: 020 7371 9300

www.thewi.org.uk

The Learning and Work Institute

www.learningandwork.org.uk

Tel: 020 7582 7221

National Trust

Tel: 0344 800 1895

www.nationaltrust.org.uk

Open University (OU)

www.open.ac.uk

Age UK

0800 678 1602

www.ageuk.org.uk

Ramblers' Association

2nd Floor Camelford House

87-90 Albert Embankment

London

SE1 7TW

Tel: 020 73961 3300

www.ramblers.org.uk

Ramblers Scotland

Caledonia House

1 Redheughs Rigg

South Gyle

Edinburgh

EH12 9DQ

Tel: 0131 357 5850

Email: scotland@ramblers.org.uk

Ramblers Cymru

3 Coopers Yard

Curran Road

Cardiff
CF10 5NB
Tel: 029 2064 6890
Email: cerddwyr@ramblers.org.uk

The Age Employment Network (TAEN)

Shaw Trust,
Third Floor, 10 Victoria Street,
Bristol,
BS1 6BN.
www.shaw-trust.org.uk

Voluntary Service Overseas (VSO)

100 London Road,
Kingston-Upon-Thames,
KT2 6QJ,
United Kingdom
020 8780 7500
www.vsointernational.org

Walking Women

Walking Women Ltd,
Scotia Works,
Leadmill Road,
Sheffield (UK),
S1 4SE
Tel: 0114 241 2774
www.walkingwomen.com

NCVO (Working for a Charity)
Society Buildings
8 All Saints Street
London N1 9RL
020 7520 2414 www.ncvo.org.uk

RUNNING YOUR HOME

Abbeyfield Society
The Abbeyfield Society,
St Peter's House,
2 Bricket Road,
St Albans,
Herts,
AL1 3JW
01727 857 536
www.abbeyfield.com

Almshouse Association
Billingbear Lodge
Maidenhead Road
Wokingham
Berkshire RG40 5RU
Tel: 01344 452922 www.almshouses.org

Pet Travel Scheme(PETS)
www.gov.uk/take-pet-abroad/overview

Disabled Living Foundation
Disabled Living Foundation,
Unit 1, 34 Chatfield Road,
Wandsworth,

London
SW11 3SE
www.dlf.org.uk
Tel: 020 7289 6111

**Elderly Accommodation
Counsel (EAC)**
3rd Floor
89 Albert Embankment
London SE1 7TP
www.housingcare.org

**Federation of Master
Builders (FMB)**
David Croft House
25 Ely Place
London, EC1N 6TD
Tel: 0330 333 7777
www.fmb.org.uk

**Foundations (the national co-ordinating
Body for home improvement agencies)**
Tel: 0300 124 0315
www.foundations.uk.com

Trust Mark
Arena Business Centre
The Square
Basing View
Basingstoke RG21 4EB
0333 555 1234
www.trustmark.org.uk
150

STAYING HEALTHY

AgeWell UK
Rounds Green Library,
Martley Road,
Oldbury,
West Midlands B69 1DZ
T: 0121 796 9333
F: 0121 217 0025
E: info@agewelluk.org.uk
www.agewell.org.uk

Arthritis Care
Helpline: 0800 5200 520
www.athritiscare.org.uk

Breast Cancer Care
www.breastcancercare.org.ul
0808 800 6000

British Dental (Oral) Health Foundation
Tel: 01788 546345
www.dentalhealth.org.uk

Diabetes UK
Wells Lawrence House,
126 Back Church Lane, London E1 1FH
Tel: 0345 123 2399
Fax: 020 7424 1001
www.diabetes.org.uk

Institute of Trichologists
107 Trinity Road
Upper Tooting
London
SW17 7SQ
Telephone: 0845 604 4657
www.trichologists.org.uk

Keep Fit Association
14 Graylands Estate, Langhurstwood Road,
Horsham,
West Sussex, RH12 4QD
Tel: 01403 266000
www.keepfit.org.uk

**Royal Osteoporosis
Society (NOS)**
Manor Farm
Skinners Hill Camerton Bath BA2 OPJ
Helpline: 0808 800 0035
www.theros.org.uk

NHS Choices advice
www.nhs.uk

Patients Association
0208 423 8999
www.patients-association.org.uk

**Royal National Institute of
BLIND People (RNIB)**
105 Judd Street

London WC1H 9NE

0303 123 9999

www.rnib.org.uk

**Royal National Institute for
Deaf People (RNID) (Action on Hearing Loss)**

Information Line: 0808 808 0123

www.actiononhearingloss.org.uk

DEVELOPING-RELATIONSHIPS

British Association for Counselling and Psychotherapy (BACP)

BACP House

15 St John's Business Park

Lutterworth

Leicestershire LE17 4HB

Tel: 01455 883300

www.bacp.co.uk

Humanists UK

Humanists UK,

39 Moreland Street,

London

EC1V 8BB.

0207 324 3060

www.humanism.org.uk

Carers UK

20 Great Dover Street

London SE1 4LX

Carersline: 0808 808 7777

www.carersuk.org

Cruse-Bereavement Care
PO Box 800
Richmond
Surrey TW9 1RG
Helpline: 0808 808 1677
www.cruse.org.uk

Family Rights Group
2nd Floor
The Print House
18 Ashwin Street
London E8 3DL
0808 801 0366
www.frg.org.uk

Grandparents' Plus
0300 123 7015
www.grandparentsplus.org.uk

Relate
Tel: 0300 003 0396
www.relate.org.uk

**United Kingdom Home
Care Association (UKHCA)**
020 8661 8188
www.ukhca.co.uk

Royal Voluntary Service
0330 555 0310
www.royalvoluntaryservice.org.uk

Index

Abbeyfield houses, 32
Activity holidays, 16
Adapting your home, 38, 53
Additional Voluntary Contributions, 138
Advice schemes, 139
Age Concern, 10, 15, 18, 22, 36, 50, 147
Almshouses, 31
Annual allowance, 103, 126, 129, 131, 133
Association of British Correspondence Colleges, 12
Association of British Insurers, 21
Attendance Allowance, 42, 58, 61
Auto Enrolment, 97

Basic lifetime annuities, 123
Bereavement allowance, 116
Bereavement payment, 116
British Association for Sexual and Relationship Therapy, 9
British Trust for Conservation Volunteers, 17
Budgeting Loan, 52

Camping, 20
Capital Gains Tax, 72, 111
Caravanning, 20
Care and Repair, 50, 53
Care in the home, 55
Chartered Surveyor Voluntary Service, 50
Citizens Advice, 139
Citizens Advice Bureau, 15, 22, 36, 50
City and Guilds, 11
Codicils, 77
Commercial property, 108, 110
Common-law marriage, 75

Community Care Grant, 52
Council Tax Benefit, 42
Cyclists Touring Club, 17

Death after retirement, 117
Defined benefit, 101
Defined contribution, 101
Dependants, 105, 116
Digital Unite, 10
Disabled facilities grant, 38, 52
Disabled Living Foundation, 39, 53, 149
Distance learning, 11

Elderly Accommodation Council, 25, 29, 31
Enduring Power of Attorney, 78
Equity release schemes, 40
Estate agents fees, 45
European Health Insurance Card, 21
Executor, 77

Federation of Master Builders, 36
Federation of Master Builders (FMB), 51
Fees, 112
Financial Conduct Authority, 140
Financial Services Authority, 104, 107
Flexi-access drawdown, 127
Flexible retirement income,, 120
Foundations, 50
Fraud, 115
Fraud Compensation Scheme., 115

Galleries, 10

Health, 21, 48, 145, 151
Holidays for carers, 23
Home Improvement Agency, 50, 51
Home Improvement Trust, 53
Home swapping, 19
Housing Options for Older People, 25
How to claim state pension, 136

Improvements, 35
Income based jobseekers allowance, 52
Income drawdown, 104
Income needs in retirement, 87
Income Support, 52
Income Tax, 64
Individual Budgets, 58
Individual Savings Account (ISA, 99
Inflation, 88, 125
Inheritance tax, 76
Inheritance Tax, 73
Insurance, 21, 145
Insurance company funds, 108
Internet, 10, 11, 18, 30, 35
Investment trusts, 108
Investment-linked annuities, 123, 124, 125
Investments, 107, 128

Land Registry, 45
Lasting Powers of Attorney, 79
Learn Direct, 11
Learning opportunities, 9
Leasehold Advisory Service, 28
Leaving the country, 136
Libraries, 9

Lifetime allowance, 126, 131
Lifetime annuity, 120
Lifetime lease, 29
Lifetime mortgages, 40
Limits to benefits and contributions, 103
Long-stay holidays, 18
Lump sum death benefits, 118

Making a will, 75
Making a Will, 3, 75
MasterBond Warranty, 51
Masters and Johnson, 8
Medical care abroad, 20
Museums, 10

National Association For Voluntary and Community action, 15
National Extension College, 12
National Federation of Women's Institutes, 14
National House Building Council, 27
National Insurance, 96
National Savings, 108
National trust, 14
NHS Prescriptions, 48
NHS sight tests, 48

Occupational pensions, 96
Occupational Therapists, 53
Office of the Public Guardian, 79
Open and Distance Learning Quality Council, 12
Open College of Arts, 12
Open Ended Investment Companies (OEICs, 110

Passport, 48

Pension credit, 52

Pension Credit, 42

Pension Credit Guarantee, 58

Pension Protection Fund, 114

Pension Tracing Service, 115

Pension-led funding, 112

Pensions, 3, 142

Pensions Advisory Services (TPAS), 139

Pensions Regulator, 135

Planning ahead for care, 63

Power of attorney, 77

Protecting pensions, 95

RADAR, 22

Radio, 10

REACH, 15

Relate, 7, 14, 154

Removal costs, 45

Repairs, 35

Retired and Senior Volunteer Programme, 15

Retirement due to ill-health, 113

Retirement housing, 25, 26, 59

Retirement options, 120

Reversion schemes, 41

Right to buy, 30

Salvation Army, 14

Scams, 140

Self-employed, 97

Self-invested Personal Pensions (SIPPs), 107

Selling your home, 43

SERPS, 95

Sexual relations, 7

Shared ownership housing, 29
Sheltered housing, 54, 59
Small Self-Administered Schemes (Ssas), 110
Social fund, 52
Social services, 52, 53
Sources of pension, 95
Special-interest holidays, 16
Specialist tour operators, 18
Stakeholder pension, 97
Stakeholder schemes, 97
Stamp duty land tax, 45
State second pension (S2P, 95
Staying Put, 50
Stock Exchange, 111

Taking a pension, 104, 113
Tax, 3, 42, 143, 144
Tax free lump sum, 103
Tax relief, 126, 129, 131, 133
Television, 10
Television licence, 49
The annual allowance, 103
The Crown, 75
The Financial Assistance Scheme, 114
The Law Society, 76
The lifetime allowance, 101
The Pension Protection Fund, 114
The Pension Tracing Service, 115
The state pension, 95
Theft, 115
Traded endowment policies, 108
Travel, 17, 34, 144, 149

TrustMark, 37, 51, 52

Uncrystallised funds, 105
University of the Third Age, 11
Unmarried partners, 75

Victim Support, 14

Voluntary Services Overseas, 20
Widowed Parent's Allowance, 116
Will-making kit, 76
Wills, 75
Women's clubs, 14
Worker Educational Associations, 11

*****